D0675360

Red
Chile
Bible

Red Chile Bible

Southwestern Classic & Gourmet Recipes

Kathleen Hansel & Audrey Jenkins

Clear Light Publishers
Santa Fe, New Mexico

Copyright © 1998 by Kathleen Hansel and Audrey Jenkins

All rights reserved. No part of this book may be reproduced or transmitted in any form or by any means, electronic or mechanical, including photocopying and recording, or by any information storage or retrieval systems without permission in writing from the publisher.

Clear Light Publishers
823 Don Diego
Santa Fe, New Mexico 87505
WEB: www.clearlightbooks.com

Library of Congress Cataloging-in-Publication Data

Hansel, Kathleen
    The red chile bible : southwestern classic & gourmet recipes / Kathleen
    Hansel & Audrey Jenkins.
            p. cm.
        ISBN 0-940666-93-6 (pbk.)
        1. Cookery (Hot peppers). 2. Hot peppers.
        3. Cookery, American—Southwestern style.
        I. Jenkins, Audrey. II. Title.

TX803.P46H36 1998   97-3648
641.6'384—dc21   CIP

First Edition
10 9 8 7 6 5 4 3

Back Cover Painting: *La Roja*, poster 1995 © R. C. Gorman

Clear Light Publishers
Santa Fe, New Mexico

Printed in U.S.A.

Contents

Acknowledgments   6

Introduction   7

Fundamentals   9

Sauces, Salsas, and Relish   19

Appetizers   31

Soups and Stews   45

Salads   57

Vegetables   67

Eggs and Cheese   79

Fish and Shellfish   91

Poultry   103

Meats   113

Pasta, Beans, and Rice   123

Breads   135

Desserts   143

Where to Buy Chiles   154

Recipe List   156

About the Authors   161

Acknowledgments

This little book owes its existence to Susan Curtis, the dynamic founder and director of the Santa Fe School of Cooking. I met Susan and joined the staff of the School in 1995, and learned more about buying, storing and cooking with chile products in the next year than I had in the previous decade. I could not have undertaken this project without her encouragement, and we could not have completed it without her expertise and support, and her stock of the best variety of red chiles in New Mexico.

We are grateful to our immensely patient publishers, and to editor Sara Held and her talent for simplifying the bafflingly complex, eliminating the redundant, and otherwise making these recipes more accessible and enjoyable for the chile novice.

We appreciate the working chefs and other good cooks who gave us inspiration, ideas and advice.

Finally, of course, we thank our friends and family members, the tireless tasters who ate their way from appetizers to dessert with unfailing good cheer—well, almost unfailing. And we promise not to cook anything with red chile in it for a month.

Introduction

The average American's relationships with food have been revolutionized in the last twenty years by a new awareness of nutrition and health, by the amazing profusion of exotic foods now available in almost every part of the country, and by a surge of creative innovation that seems to move directly from the restaurant kitchen to the home kitchen without skipping a beat. On the go, we are dining out at restaurants more and cooking at home less. And when we do choose to cook at home, we are more likely to be inspired by the latest glossy food magazine or the great Thai restaurant we went to on our last out-of-town trip than by memories of Mom's macaroni and cheese! We grew up with television and (one way or another) have traveled the country and the world, including its remote and rustic places. As citizens of the "global village," we have brought everybody's food traditions home to our American kitchens, and we're busy translating them in new ways.

One of the greatest of those traditions is chile, the charismatic capsicum that fires up local cuisines from Chihuahua to Calcutta to Canton. Today, the mention of chile may still conjure in the mind a bowl of red beef stew with beans that burns the mouth and clears the sinuses, but we know that is only part of the story. American cooks are born designers—creative people who love a challenge and are naturally inclined to experimentation, respectfully regarding other people's traditions as their own jumping off points. How exciting that today we're prepared to enjoy the surprising and delicious combination of chiles with creamy blue cheese, with sweet fresh peaches, even with buttery chocolate cake!

In this little book, we have included recipes from the very traditional to the very contemporary, from down-home rustic to elegant indeed, and from comfortably mellow to fiery hot. Most of the dishes have roots in Mexico or the American Southwest, but we've also included some distinctly Asian treatments.

We share the modern cook's commitment to healthy foods, natural flavors, and (not least) a creative cooking experience. We tend to cook by the seasons, because usually the true, best flavor and quality of the produce can only be obtained when it comes straight from local farms and gardens. Accordingly, our recipes rely extensively on fresh ingredients and often are built "from scratch." But we're also acutely aware that time itself is in short supply for many cooks, and we certainly encourage whatever shortcuts and substitutions you usually make to save preparation time at a minimum sacrifice of quality or flavor. We routinely substitute frozen corn, for example, if it's out of season or we only have ten minutes to get the corn pudding in the oven! If you're new to the world of chiles, be very careful in substituting one kind for another or powder for puree (see Fundamentals), but follow your good cooking instincts with respect to other ingredients.

Above all, be creative and have a good time! We have always regarded recipes as guidelines and starting points—and if you love to cook, you probably do, too. We hope you will have as much fun cooking with these recipes as we had putting them together.

The Fundamentals

The last decade has seen an explosion of culinary interest in all things "hot," and there is an expanding array of commercially prepared hot sauces, salsas, pickled and preserved chiles, and chile powders available in supermarkets and specialty stores throughout the country. Most of us rely extensively on these wonderful chile preparations, because they are easy and convenient and suit our busy lifestyles. Nevertheless, buying, storing, and preparing fresh and dried chile peppers is really quite simple, and anyone who cooks can add a variety of powerful home-made chile preparations to the larder with relatively little effort.

For us, it's fun to work "from scratch" to create our own chile con-coctions, and to experiment with mixtures of different chiles. For this book, we have used only a few of the many kinds of red chiles—the ones we believe are most widely available across the country, and available by mail or telephone order from sources listed at the back of this book. Naturally, if you enjoy cooking and have some familiarity with chiles, you will substitute your own favorite chiles, or introduce new and exotic chiles to your repertoire, or mix different chiles and proportions of chiles to see what happens. We've never met a recipe we didn't want to play with, and we encourage even chile beginners to be just as creative with chiles as they are with their other favorite foods.

Substituting amounts of chile or kinds of chiles in a recipe can be a little risky, however, until you become familiar with the different heat levels you can expect. A little capsaicin goes a long way for folks new to the pungent joys of fiery food! Tossing an extra serrano chile into a salsa, for example, or substituting a habanero for a jalapeño, can render the final product inedible for those who have yet to develop the charac-teristic cast-iron stomach of the seasoned chile lover. We have indicated low-risk substitutions below in our descriptions of the red chiles used in this book. Remember, also, that most of the heat-producing capsaicin of the chile is concentrated in the seeds and veins. Virtually all our recipes call for removing the seeds and veins; but if you want more heat in the dish without adding more chiles or substituting a hotter variety, try including the seeds and veins in the dish.

Caution: When working with hot chiles, it is best to wear plastic gloves and to wash your hands thoroughly as soon as you're done. *Never* touch your eyes, nose or face after working with chiles until you have removed all traces of capsaicin from your hands. We scrub hands and nails (with a brush) in a solution of soap and warm water, and then rinse in a basin of cold water mixed with a tablespoon of liquid bleach.

Fresh Red Chiles

Virtually all chile varieties start off green, but fully ripened chiles may be yellow, orange, red, purple, even white! The few fresh red chiles we have used in these recipes are the fully ripened stage of chile varieties that are more commonly harvested and used while still green. Most of the ripened crop is dried and sold as pods or powder, and red chile really comes into its own in the sauces and stews based on the dried product. Generally, fully ripened red chile has a sweeter, richer flavor while the green stage yields a crisper, vegetable flavor. In many recipes calling for fresh red chiles (particularly raw salsas and salads), the fresh green stage of the same chile can be substituted if necessary—just remember that not only the color but the flavor will be different.

New Mexico Red is the fully ripened stage of the New Mexico green chile, 6 to 8 inches long and up to 2 inches wide. It is a deep red color, with rich, sweet flavor and medium to medium-high heat. It is not widely available in its fresh form outside the Southwest, where it is only abundant for a brief period at the end of the fall harvest. Most of the New Mexico chile crop is grown in the southern part of the state, and Hatch, New Mexico is regarded here as the chile capital of the world. But for red chiles, we personally prefer the Chimayó chiles grown in the mountain valleys of the Sangre de Cristo range north of Santa Fe. New Mexico red chiles may be roasted, peeled, and used to make red sauces and salsas; but they are more commonly sun-dried for use throughout the winter months, or strung into *ristras* for decorative purposes.

*Substitute: **Anaheim Red**,* the fully ripened stage of the Anaheim green chile, a mild-mannered cousin of the New Mexico chile. The Anaheim is 5 to 7 inches long and about 1½ inches wide. When ripe it is a fire-engine red color, with mild flavor and very mild to medium heat.

Red Jalapeño is the fully ripe stage of the popular little green chile so widely available pickled en escabeche in American grocery stores from

Hoboken to Seattle. The fresh red jalapeño is about 2 inches long and 1½ inches in diameter at the shoulders, tapering slightly to a point. It is a bright red chile, medium hot with a fresh, crisp flavor that is great for fresh salsas and salads. Red jalapeños are available for much of the year in the Southwest and California, and red jalapeño powder is also available from many sources.

Substitute: **Red Fresno**, a little hotter; or **Red Serrano**, much hotter so cut down the amount used.

Red Fresno chiles look so much like jalapeños they are often confused. The Fresno is about 2½ inches long and 1½ to 2 inches in diameter at the shoulders, tapering slightly to a point. It is a clear red, thick-fleshed chile, hot to very hot. It is excellent in fresh salsas and salads, and we use it interchangeably with red jalapeños for many recipes, although it has more heat.

Substitute: **Red Jalapeño**, not quite as hot; **Red Serrano**, a little hotter so cut down the amount used.

Red Serrano is the brilliant red, fully ripened stage of the green serrano. It is nearly cylindrical, about 2 inches long and ½ inch in diameter from stem to stern. Most of the serrano crops are picked and sold green, then used fresh or pickled en escabeche for use throughout the year. Fresh red serranos have a crisp, clear flavor and are hot to very hot.

Substitute: **Red Fresno**, not quite as hot; **Red Jalapeño**, much milder so increase the amount used.

Buying and Storing Fresh Red Chiles

We buy and store fresh chiles exactly the same way we do tomatoes. We find that chiles and bell peppers typically look better a week after we buy them than tomatoes, but are losing vitality with each passing day! Remember that fresh red chiles are fully ripened, and even under the best conditions they will not "keep" as long as fresh green chiles of the same varieties. At the market, select firm chiles that are heavy and have a fresh smell. The skins should be dry, shiny, and smooth without pits or blemishes that could indicate rot, and without any signs of shriveling that could indicate they are past their prime and either rotting inside or drying out.

Depending on your climate, you may be able to store fresh red chiles at home with relatively little deterioration for up to a week before using them. The important thing is to provide the best temperature, moisture, and light conditions you can. We find that fresh chiles, like fresh tomatoes, don't take very well to plastic bags or refrigerators—so we avoid refrigeration if we can.

In the arid southwestern climate, fresh chiles can begin to wrinkle and dry immediately. We recommend storing fresh chiles for up to a week in brown paper sacks (open at the top for air circulation) in a dark basement where the air is relatively cooler and moister than in the kitchen. If you live in a hot, dry climate and don't have a basement, you can wrap the chiles in paper towels, seal them into a plastic bag, and store them in the refrigerator. If you live in a very humid climate, you can probably store fresh chiles in open paper sacks on a kitchen shelf for a week or more if your house is air conditioned. If your kitchen conditions are hot and damp, however, you may have to resort to refrigeration or the chiles will begin to rot quickly. Whatever your storage conditions, try to use fresh chiles in three to five days, or roast, peel, and freeze them while they are still in top condition.

Roasting Fresh Chiles

Skins of fresh chiles and bell peppers are the most indigestible part when cooked, and should generally be charred and removed unless the chiles or peppers are to be used raw. The object of roasting is to blister and blacken the skin of the chile quickly all over without cooking the tender flesh to a pulp. Always select firm, fresh chiles with smooth, shiny skins and no dark spots or other signs of aging. The charring process will release strong fumes loaded with capsaicin into the air! We think the fragrance is wonderful, but it can cause sneezing and stinging eyes, too—so be certain you have good ventilation, and keep your face averted as you turn the chiles.

Using a hot, open flame is the very best method for charring the skins off chiles, and some professional chefs use a propane torch for the job. Our preferred technique is to set a small, sturdy, narrow-gauge grill rack directly over the full-blast gas flame of the kitchen range, and when the rack is hot set the chiles on the rack and char them over the flames as quickly as possible, turning with tongs to blacken them evenly (about 10 minutes overall). If you have an electric range, you can set the rack directly over the heating element, set the element on high, and when the rack is hot set the chiles on the rack to char. Don't let the chiles rest directly on the heating element. If you prefer to use the oven broiler, preheat it and set the chiles on the broiler rack 1 or 2 inches below the flame or heating element, then turn them with tongs until they are charred. Leave the broiler door open. We don't use the broiler because it's a hassle to keep an eye on progress by pulling the rack in and out, and because the buildup of heat inside the oven can cook the chiles too much.

Once the chiles are charred, remove them from the rack to a plastic bag, or to a glass bowl covered tightly with plastic wrap, and let them "sweat" for 10 or 15 minutes until they are cool enough to handle. The skins will then pull off fairly easily, depending on the type of chile. The ease of pulling the charred skins off under running water is tempting, but you do lose some of the juices and roasted flavor if you take that shortcut. If you plan to stuff the chiles, leave the stems intact and make a single slit down the length of the chile to remove the seeds and veins; otherwise, just stem, seed and devein the chiles with a sharp knife. Roasted chiles will keep in the refrigerator for a few days, but should be frozen for longer storage.

When we roast a lot of fresh chiles at once for later use, we lay out the charred chiles on a baking sheet in their skins and freeze them, then seal them into plastic freezer bags for storage so we can pull them out individually as needed for use in cooked salsas, sauces, and other cooked dishes. Fresh roasted chiles will keep well in a deep freeze for up to a year if they are well sealed, but we would not recommend keeping them in the freezer compartment of a home refrigerator for more than a few months. After the chiles are thawed, the skins slip off easily. It is possible to stuff roasted chiles that have been frozen, but we have more success with frozen chiles rellenos if we roast, peel, and stuff them *before* freezing.

Dried Red Chiles

A wide variety of dried red chiles is increasingly available in major metropolitan areas throughout the country in the form of whole pods, pods crushed into flakes (chile Caribe) or pure powder. For these recipes, we have included seven basic chile varieties that are most commonly used in Mexican and southwestern cooking.

A word about **ristras:** In the Southwest, almost every home sports at least one charming ristra of red chiles strung together in 2- to 3-foot swags and hung at the front door, on the porch, or in the kitchen for decoration. And ristras are among the most popular mementos of a visit to the Southwest. If they have dried properly, red chile pods can be pulled from the ristra for use in the cooking pot. However, the best pods for cooking have been individually and uniformly sun-dried, then carefully preserved free from exposure to dust, insects, light, humidity, or temperature fluctuations. We recommend using ristras for decoration, and buying and storing properly prepared pods for cooking.

New Mexico Red is the fully ripened, then dried New Mexico chile. Dried, the pods shrink to 5 to 6 inches long and about 1½ inches wide. Fully dried, the pod is a deep, ruby-red color with a smooth, shiny skin, an earthy, sweet flavor, and medium to medium-high heat. We use pods, flakes (chile Caribe, which includes the seeds), and pure powder for recipes in this book. For powder, we prefer the Chimayó chiles grown in the mountain valleys north of Santa Fe, obtainable from the Santa Fe School of Cooking. Dried New Mexico red chile is a year-round staple for the red sauces, soups, stews, tamales, and posoles of New Mexico.

Substitute: **Chile Colorado**, the dried pods of the red Anaheim chile, generally milder in both flavor and heat level. The dried pods are 4 to 5 inches long and about 1 inch wide, a deep but bright red color, with mild flavor and very mild to medium heat.

Ancho chiles are dried poblano chiles, one of the three most popular Mexican chiles for cooking. Anchos are a very dark mahogany color and very wrinkled, 3 to 5 inches long, up to 3 inches wide at the stem end, and rounded at the bottom. Anchos have mild to medium heat and a very rich, sweet flavor. They are widely available whole, and available in pure powdered form from some sources.

Substitute: **Mulato** (milder); **Pasilla** (smokier).

Mulato is another form of dried poblano. It is about the same size but has a more tapered shape and its wrinkled skin is generally darker, almost to black in color. The flavor of mulatos is not as rich or long-lasting, and it has a very mild heat rating.

Substitute: **Ancho; Pasilla.**

Pasilla chiles (sometimes called chile negro) are dried chilaca chiles. They are very dark brown, almost black in color, have a very wrinkly skin, and are typically 5 to 6 inches long and about 1 inch wide. They have mild to medium heat, and a unique, rich, slightly smoky flavor that we think is unmistakable. They are excellent for sauces. Along with the ancho, it is a staple chile of Mexican cooking.

Note: Even in the Southwest, ancho or mulato chiles are sometimes labeled "pasilla" chiles, so it is worthwhile to learn to recognize the long, thin pasillas by sight and not rely on packaging to be sure you're getting the right chile. Pasilla chiles are also available powdered.

Substitute: **Mulato; Ancho.**

Guajillo chiles are shiny, deep red pods, about 1½ inches wide and 4 to 6 inches long, tapered to a point. They have a sweet flavor and mild to medium heat. Guajillos are a good addition to red sauces, especially with ancho or pasilla chiles.

Substitute: New Mexico Red; Chile Colorado.

Chipotles are smoked, dried jalapeño chiles with a very distinctive, campfire flavor. They are dull tan to coffee brown in color, with a very shriveled appearance, and are about 2 inches long and 1 inch across. Chipotles are medium hot to hot. Chipotles are available whole, or ground into powder; but we find that canned or bottled chipotles *en adobo* (that is, chipotles that have been rehydrated and then pickled in a tomato-based sauce) are the most convenient form of chipotle chile for most cooking.

Substitute: There really is no substitute for chipotles. You can always add chile heat to any dish by adding any kind of hot chile, but the unique, smoky flavor of chipotles can be had only by using chipotles! Many dishes calling for chipotle chiles are also wonderful made with pasilla chiles—but, of course, they have an entirely different chile flavor.

Cayenne chiles are translucent, bright red chiles, 2 to 4 inches long and up to a half inch across, with very pungent heat. Cayenne chile is most familiar and widely available in powdered form. *Chile de arbol*, another small, hot chile, is popular in the Southwest and we use the two chiles interchangeably.

Substitute: Chile de Arbol, Chile Pulla.

Pequin chiles are fiery little chiles about ½ inch long and ¼ inch wide. They are orange-red with smooth skins and are very intensely hot—use with discretion!

Substitute: Chile Cayenne or *Chile de Arbol*, both a little milder.

Buying and Storing Dried Red Chiles

An increasing array of dried chiles is available in most large metropolitan areas, and many specialty suppliers make a variety of whole dried chiles and chile powders available by mail order (see our list of suppliers at the back of the book). Kept in dark, cool, fairly arid conditions, dried chile pods and powders can retain their flavor and freshness almost indefinitely. However, we treat them the same way we do other dried herbs and spices: we toss out what's left after 6 months to a year on the shelf, and start fresh! We follow the same rule for dried chiles that have been rehydrated and then pickled en escabeche or en adobo (such as chipotles en adobo), keeping the opened jar or bottle in the refrigerator for up to a year, then tossing it out and opening a new one. We also rehydrate dried chiles and turn them into purees so they are instantly available for cooking, yet still amenable to long-term storage. Chile puree will keep several months in the refrigerator covered with a film of olive oil, or up to a year in the freezer.

Drying intensifies the flavors of chiles, and concentrates the pungent capsaicin, so both flavor and heat are readily available from dried chile pods and powders that have been properly preserved. Whole dried chile pods are best when still slightly flexible and aromatic, but crackling dry pods are still perfectly good for cooking so long as they have retained their color and integrity. Shop for dried chile pods the same way you shop for any vegetable product you plan to cook and eat! Choose chiles that are whole, clean, uniform in color, and close to the same size. Reject chiles that are broken, faded or spotted, dusty or dirty, or show any evidence of insect infestation. Store dried chiles in airtight containers in a cool, dry place away from light, and check on unused chiles every month or so to be certain they are not molding, spotting, breaking up, or suddenly hosting a family of enterprising moths. If you live in a very humid climate, you may have to store your airtight container in the refrigerator.

Buying Chile Powders

When buying chile powders, select *pure chile powders*—not "chili" seasoning powders, which usually contain a variety of other spices and ingredients from dehydrated garlic powder to sugar and artificial colorings. Buy powder that is slightly lumpy, an indication that the natural oils have not evaporated, and store it in an airtight container in a cool, dark, dry place.

Preparing Chile Purees

Dried red chile pods must be cleaned, rehydrated, and cooked before we can enjoy them in our food. Typically, Mexican cooks begin the process of preparing dried chiles by toasting them on a comal or frying them in oil before rehydrating them. Many American cooks omit the toasting and begin the preparation with rehydrating the chiles. In a hectic world, however, we find it most convenient to reach into the refrigerator for the chile puree we have already prepared! We make it in batches using 6 to 10 chiles at a time, and the yield varies by the kind of chile we're using (that is, the size of the pod), and how much water we add. We find that for our most-used dried chiles (New Mexico, ancho, mulato, and pasilla) we get up to 1 tablespoon of thick puree per large chile pod.

To make puree, first wipe the chiles with a damp cloth to remove any dust. Break the stems off the chiles and shake out the seeds, or break open the pods and remove the seeds and veins. Scatter the chiles into a dry skillet over medium-high heat and dry roast them for 2 or 3 minutes, stirring or turning the pieces so they will not scorch. Then put the chiles into a small bowl and pour boiling water over them just to cover (generally about 1 cup of boiling water will cover 6 to 8 medium-sized chiles), and let them soak for 20 or 30 minutes until they are completely soft. Spoon the chiles out of the soaking water with a slotted spoon or strainer and put them in a blender jar. Then taste the soaking liquid—if it is very bitter, throw it out; otherwise reserve it. Pulse the chiles to a puree in the blender, adding as much soaking water (or additional water, if you had to discard the soaking water) as needed to make a thick puree.

To store the puree, scrape it out of the blender into a clean glass jar, float a thick film of olive oil over the top to seal the puree from any exposure to air, cover the jar tightly, and store in the refrigerator for up to several months. We also on occasion spoon chile puree into oiled ice cube trays (2 tablespoons per "cube"), freeze the trays, then pop out the frozen cubes into a plastic freezer bag for long-term storage.

Sauces, Salsas, and Relish

Chile-Cherry Glaze

This sweet and spicy glaze is wonderful for baked hams, pork roasts, and roasted fowl.

½ lb. ripe, sweet cherries, pitted
(or frozen pitted cherries)
1½ cups red chile honey
3 Tbs. fresh lime juice

2 tsp. lime zest
1 fresh red jalapeño chile,
    seeded and minced
3 Tbs. cilantro, chopped

Mince the sweet cherries, or thaw the frozen cherries and drain, reserving juice; then mince. In a medium saucepan, combine all the ingredients (and reserved cherry juice, if any) and bring to a simmer over medium-low heat. Reduce heat to low, and simmer the mixture until it becomes thick and syrupy. Remove from the heat and cool slightly. Makes about 1½ cups of glaze.

Chile Caribe Rub

Use this hot rub to marinate meats or fish filets for grilling or skillet blackening. If you like, grind 2 teaspoons of rub into a paste with a fresh garlic clove before using—it adds fresh garlic flavor and helps the dry rub adhere to and penetrate the meat. You can also use it to pep up salad dressings and sauces.

1 large very dry New Mexico
    red chile
2 tsp. mild Chimayó chile powder
2 tsp. dried thyme, crushed
2 tsp. dried Mexican oregano,
    crushed
2 tsp. cumin seed, toasted
    and crushed

1 tsp. coriander seed,
    toasted and ground
1 tsp. ground cloves
1 tsp. ground cinnamon
1 to 2 tsp. turbinado
    or dark brown sugar
1 tsp. salt

Wipe the chile with a barely damp cloth to remove any dirt or dust. Remove the stem (but not the seeds) and break up the chile into a mortar or stone bowl. Crush the chile thoroughly. In a deep bowl, gently stir the crushed red chile with the remaining ingredients to blend, taking care not to bring your face close to the bowl or inhale any of the mixture. Carefully spoon the rub into a glass jar, cover tightly, and wash your hands thoroughly. Store the rub away from light in a cool, dry place. It will keep well for years if you have used fresh ingredients and the jar is not exposed to light or moisture (the refrigerator is cool and dark, but full of moisture). If you don't have a cool, dry place to store the jar, try sealing the rub into a plastic freezer bag and keeping it frozen.

Sweet Chipotle Vegetable Relish

This sweet, fiery relish complements grilled meats. Add a couple of fresh, diced apples and a handful of salted pecans to the finished relish and serve it on mixed greens as a zesty salad.

1 lb. young carrots, sliced
   1/4-inch thick
1 lb. zucchini, quartered lengthwise,
   sliced 1/4-inch thick
15 pearl onions
1/2 green bell pepper, minced
1/2 medium onion, minced
1 cup tomato or V-8 juice
1/2 Tbs. pureed chipotle en adobo,
   or to taste

1/2 cup brown sugar
1/3 cup cider vinegar
2 Tbs. white wine vinegar
4 Tbs. olive oil
1 Tbs. Worcestershire Sauce
1 Tbs. dark brown mustard
1 Tbs. dark soy sauce
1 tsp. salt

Steam the carrots and zucchini just until tender-crunchy, 3 or 4 minutes, and plunge them in ice water; when cool, drain and set aside. Bring a pot of water to a rolling boil, drop the pearl onions into the pot for 10 or 20 seconds to loosen skins; plunge into cold water, and peel. Steam the onions 2 or 3 minutes, just until tender-crunchy, plunge into cold water to cool, drain, and set aside.

Whisk the remaining ingredients in a heavy saucepan and bring to a boil over medium heat. Simmer on low for 30 minutes, stirring frequently. Let the marinade cool 10 or 15 minutes, pour the warm marinade over the steamed vegetables in a deep glass bowl, and cool to room temperature; then cover and refrigerate. Marinate the relish for 2 to 5 days, stirring several times a day. Drain and serve. Makes about 1 quart.

Red Chile Ginger Gremolata

Lovers of Italian food are familiar with a piquant relish of fresh minced garlic, parsley, and lemon zest called gremolata. This Southwest-style gremolata adds heat and crunchy textural interest to cream soups and slow-cooked stews, and can be served with grilled beef, chicken, and fish instead of a sauce. Easy to mince together at the last minute, it can be made with whatever chiles, herbs, fruits, and nuts you have on hand.

1 Tbs. fresh ginger, finely minced
1 Tbs. fresh red jalapeño or
    Fresno chile, seeded and minced
2 Tbs. scallion greens, minced

2 Tbs. red chile pecans, chopped
3 Tbs. fresh apple, peeled
    and minced

Mince and mix the ingredients immediately before serving. Makes about 1/2 cup.

Red Chile Pear Chutney

This spicy fresh chutney goes well with any curry dish or cold roasted meat.

1/2 cup white wine vinegar
1/2 cup balsamic vinegar
1/4 cup turbinado or granulated
    sugar
1 medium white onion, minced
1 fresh red jalapeño or Fresno chile,
    seeded and minced
1/2 cup raisins
4 ripe but firm pears, cored
    and diced

1/4 cup freshly squeezed lime juice
2 Tbs. grated fresh ginger
1 tsp. Chimayó chile powder,
    or to taste
1 tsp. ground cinnamon
1/2 tsp. ground cloves
1 tsp. salt
1 cup fresh parsley leaves

In a heavy, enameled saucepan, boil the vinegars with the sugar until the mixture is reduced to a thick glaze, about 15 to 20 minutes. Reduce the heat to medium-low, add the minced onion and chile, and cook 3 minutes. Add the raisins and all but 1 cup of the pears to the mixture and cook, stirring at gentle boil until the pears are cooked to a coarse puree, about 10 minutes. Remove the saucepan from the heat, stir in the lime juice until it is well combined; then stir in the ginger, chile powder, spices, salt, and parsley and let the chutney cool completely at room temperature. Stir in the reserved diced pears, spoon the mixture into a clean glass jar, cover tightly, and refrigerate. The chutney will keep about a week. Bring to room temperature before using. Makes 3 1/2 cups.

Chipotle Hollandaise Sauce

You can whip up this velvety sauce in minutes with no cooking. The mellow, smoky flavor of the chipotles goes well with poached fish, cold roasted fowl or pork loin, or roasted green vegetables. Use it right away! The longer it sits, the more fire it will develop.

3 egg yolks
3/4 cup melted butter
A large pinch of salt

1 tsp. pureed chipotle en adobo
1 Tbs. lemon juice

Set out the yolks, chipotle puree, and lemon juice in covered dishes to come to room temperature (it will take at least an hour). Heat a mixing bowl with hot water, pour out the water and add the yolks. Whip the yolks vigorously with a wire whisk for a few seconds; then very slowly drizzle the melted butter into the yolks, whipping continuously, until all the butter is absorbed and the sauce is thickened and smooth. Whip in the salt, chipotle puree, and lemon juice, and serve immediately. Makes almost two cups. (In a rush? Whip up this sauce in a blender, adding the melted butter slowly.)

🌶 🌶 🌶

Roasted Garlic Chile Mayonnaise

This is best made with your own mayonnaise, but a good bottled mayonnaise will do. It doubles as a sandwich spread and a sauce for seafood and cold vegetables.

2 whole heads of fresh, rosy garlic
1/2 tsp. balsamic vinegar
1 or 2 tsp. Chimayó chile powder
2 tsp. fresh basil, chopped

1 cup mayonnaise
Salt and freshly ground pepper,
to taste

Preheat the oven to 400 degrees. Separate the garlic cloves and wrap tightly in foil, then roast until tender, about 35 to 40 minutes. Let the garlic cool until you can handle the cloves; then peel them and put them in a blender jar. Add the remaining ingredients to the garlic and process until the mayonnaise is smooth and well blended. Taste for seasoning, and add salt and pepper or additional chile powder to taste. Makes 1 1/4 cups.

Cilantro Mint Salsa

This fresh herb and chile salsa goes well with hot or cold seafood, cold roasted chicken or pork. It can be used as a base for a tropical fruit salsa — just add ½ cup of cubed fresh pineapple, mango, papaya, or kiwi fruit.

1 bunch fresh cilantro, chopped
½ cup fresh mint, chopped
¼ cup peeled water chestnuts,
   drained and chopped
3 medium garlic cloves, minced
2 Tbs. fresh ginger, minced
1 fresh red serrano chile,
   seeded and minced
½ fresh red jalapeño chile,
   seeded and minced

1 tsp. cumin seeds, toasted
   and ground
½ tsp. coriander seeds,
   toasted and ground
½ cup virgin olive oil
⅓ cup fresh lime juice
¼ tsp. salt, or to taste

Toss all the ingredients together in a medium glass bowl and chill. Makes 1½ cups of salsa.

Dried Cherry Chipotle Relish

A sweet-hot relish for roasted pork or poultry, it is also good with lamb.

1 whole head of fresh, rosy garlic
2 Tbs. virgin olive oil
1½ cups white onion, finely
   chopped
1 cup freshly squeezed orange juice
1 cup white wine vinegar
½ cup red wine vinegar

1¼ cups turbinado or brown sugar
2½ cups dried cherries (10 oz.)
1 Tbs. chipotle in adobo, finely
   chopped (or more, to taste)
⅛ tsp. ground cumin
½ tsp. ground cinnamon

Preheat the oven to 400 degrees. Separate the garlic cloves, wrap them tightly in foil, and roast until tender, about 35 to 40 minutes. Allow the garlic to cool, peel the cloves, and set aside. Heat the olive oil in a heavy, enameled saucepan, and sauté the finely chopped onion over medium heat for about 5 minutes. Add the orange juice, vinegars, and turbinado and bring to a boil, stirring until the sugar is dissolved. Boil the mixture until reduced to about 2 cups, about 15 minutes. Add the garlic, cherries, chipotle chile, cumin, and cinnamon. Reduce the heat to medium-low and simmer, stirring frequently, until the liquid is reduced to a thin syrup, about 15 minutes. Let the relish cool at room temperature, spoon into a clean jar, cover tightly, and chill. The relish is best made several days ahead, and keeps for more than a week. Bring to room temperature before serving. Makes 2½ cups of relish.

Orange Sauce with Chiles and Ginger

This piquant but delicate sauce complements hot or cold seafood.

1 large, sweet orange
2 cups freshly squeezed
 and strained orange juice
1/2 cup dry white wine
1 fresh red jalapeño or Fresno chile,
 seeded and minced

3 Tbs. fresh ginger, finely minced
1/3 cup shallots, finely minced
3/4 cup heavy cream
Salt and ground white pepper,
 to taste

Cut the orange in half crosswise and remove the sections with a sharp knife. Put the sections in a strainer and let stand until well drained; then refrigerate. In a small heavy saucepan, boil the orange juice with the wine, minced chiles, ginger, and shallots until reduced to 3/4 cup, 30 to 40 minutes. Stir in the cream and continue to boil until reduced to about 1 cup, about 10 to 15 minutes. Remove the sauce from the heat and let cool to room temperature. Taste, and add salt and ground white pepper. Just before serving, stir in the reserved orange sections. Makes 1 1/2 cups of sauce.

Salsa Fresca

Our favorite fresh tomato salsa to serve with tortilla chips, tacos, breakfast eggs—virtually anything but dessert.

1 lb. ripe plum tomatoes, peeled,
 seeded, and chopped
2 fresh red jalapeño or red serrano
 chiles, seeded and minced
4 scallions, sliced thin
1 large garlic clove, minced

1 Tbs. fresh cilantro leaves, chopped
1/2 tsp. Mexican oregano
2 Tbs. freshly squeezed lime juice
Salt and freshly ground pepper,
 to taste

Mix all ingredients together in a glass bowl, cover, and chill. Best served within 2 days. Makes about 2 1/2 cups of salsa.

Pasilla Chile Sauce with Almonds

This typical red sauce from central Mexico, thickened with ground nuts can be used to sauce enchiladas, tacos, roasted poultry, or grilled beef—or to flavor soups and stews. It can also be made with ancho chiles, or a combination of ancho and pasilla chiles.

3 dried pasilla chiles
1 thick slice French bread
1/2 cup olive oil
1/3 cup whole blanched almonds, skinned
1/2 medium white onion, finely chopped

3 garlic cloves, roughly chopped
2 medium tomatoes, peeled, seeded, and diced
1/8 tsp. cayenne pepper, or to taste
1/2 tsp. salt
1 Tbs. wine vinegar

Wipe the chiles clean with a damp cloth, then stem and seed them. Pour 1 cup of boiling water over the chiles and let them soak 20 to 30 minutes. Drain the chiles, reserving soaking water, and dry on paper towels. Toast the French bread until dry and browned, tear into pieces, and set aside. In a heavy skillet, heat the olive oil over medium heat and sauté the chiles in the oil for 2 or 3 minutes, turning and stirring to prevent scorching. Remove the chiles to a blender or food processor. In the oil, sauté the almonds, stirring, until they are just golden, about 2 minutes, and remove them with a slotted spoon to the blender jar with the chiles. Add the onion and garlic to the hot oil and sauté for 2 minutes. Pour the onion, garlic and oil into the blender jar, and add the diced tomato, cayenne, salt, bread, and half the chile soaking liquid. Pulse the mixture, then blend until smooth and thick, adding the remaining chile soaking liquid as necessary. Pour in the vinegar and blend 20 or 30 seconds to mix.

Use the sauce immediately, or spoon into a clean jar, cover tightly, and keep in the refrigerator for up to 3 days. This very thick sauce can be thinned to desired consistency by stirring in a good vegetable or meat stock. Makes 2 1/2 cups of sauce.

Chimayó Red Sauce

This is an earthy, typically northern New Mexican red chile sauce made with 100 percent pure ground powder from dried New Mexico chiles that are grown in the high mountain valleys around Chimayó. Basic red chile sauce is an everyday staple throughout the Southwest; it is simple to make and freezes beautifully. You may want to experiment with various combinations of mild and hot powdered red chiles. We urge you, however, to use only pure ground red chile powders and not the "chili powder" products that include other ingredients such as garlic powder and herbs.

½ cup pure Chimayó chile powder
2½ cups rich vegetable broth
  (or water)
2 or 3 Tbs. canola oil
1 small white onion, finely chopped
2 cloves fresh, rosy garlic,
  finely chopped

1 tsp. cumin seed, toasted
  and ground
1 tsp. Mexican oregano
⅛ tsp. ground cinnamon
1 tsp. salt

Put the chile powder in a medium bowl and whisk 1 cup of the broth or water into the powder to make a smooth mixture with no lumps, then set aside. Heat the oil in a large, heavy saucepan and sauté the onion for 5 minutes over medium heat. Toss in the garlic and sauté another 2 minutes. Stir in the cumin, oregano, and cinnamon and cook, stirring constantly, for 2 minutes. Scrape the chile mixture into the pan and stir; then add the remaining broth or water and cook, stirring, until the sauce reaches the simmering point. Do not let the chile scorch. Reduce the heat to low, add the salt, and simmer the sauce gently, stirring frequently, for 20 to 30 minutes or until it is the consistency you like; then set aside to cool. When cool, pour into a clean jar, cover tightly, and store in the refrigerator. The sauce keeps well for up to 2 weeks. To keep it longer, freeze it as soon as it has cooled. Makes about 2 cups.

San Miguel Red Sauce

This is a typical sauce of central Mexico, made with whole dried ancho, pasilla, and mulato chiles, to be served with pork or bean stews, and roasted or grilled meats. You may want to experiment with different proportions of chile types. When buying the dried chiles for this sauce, get the freshest and most flexible available in your market.

2¹/₂ cups rich chicken or beef stock
dried chiles: 5 pasilla, 3 ancho,
   3 mulato
4 Tbs. lard
1 medium white onion, chopped
3 fresh garlic cloves, peeled and
   roughly chopped

2 Tbs. almonds, hazelnuts or piñon
   (or pine) nuts, ground
¹/₂ tsp. cumin seeds, toasted
   and ground
¹/₈ tsp. each ground cinnamon
   and cloves
¹/₂ tsp. salt

Bring the stock to a simmer, reduce heat, and keep hot. Stem and seed the chiles. In a large, heavy skillet, heat the 4 tablespoons lard and fry the chiles, turning frequently to prevent scorching, until they are very dark and have softened. Remove the chiles with a slotted spoon to a blender jar, leaving the melted lard in the skillet. Sauté the onion and garlic in the lard for 2 minutes, and remove with a slotted spoon to the blender jar with the chiles. Add ¹/₄ cup of the hot stock to the blender jar and process the chiles, onions, and garlic to a puree, adding more stock as necessary to achieve a thick but fairly smooth mixture.

Reheat the remaining lard and scrape the puree into the skillet. Fry the puree, stirring constantly to keep the chiles from scorching, for 2 or 3 minutes. Whisk the rest of the hot stock into the chile mixture, then toss in the remaining ingredients. Simmer the sauce, stirring occasionally, for 20 to 30 minutes. The sauce keeps well for up to 2 weeks. Makes about 3 cups.

Santa Cruz Red Sauce

This recipe is adapted from the fiftieth anniversary cookbook of the Santa Cruz Chili & Spice Company in Tumacacori, Arizona. Santa Cruz chiles are an Anaheim type, generally a little milder than New Mexico chiles, and are a favorite for use in enchiladas, soups, and stews in Arizona. This recipe calls for flour as a thickening agent.

$^1/_2$ cup Santa Cruz Chili Paste
$^1/_3$ cup Santa Cruz Chili Powder
$2^1/_2$ cups rich beef broth
$^1/_3$ cup lard or shortening
1 small white onion, finely chopped
1 tsp. cumin seed, toasted
   and ground

1 tsp. Mexican oregano
$^2/_3$ cup flour
Salt and freshly ground black pepper,
   to taste

Put the chile paste in a heavy saucepan and whisk in the chile powder. Set the saucepan over medium heat and slowly whisk the beef broth into the chile mixture to make a smooth liquid with no lumps. Bring the chile mixture to a strong simmer, stirring frequently to prevent scorching, then reduce the heat and cook 5 minutes.

Heat the lard in a large, heavy saucepan and sauté the onion over medium-high heat for 5 minutes. Stir in the cumin and oregano and cook for 2 minutes. Sprinkle the flour over the onion mixture and whisk the mixture constantly until the flour is cooked but not browned, about 4 minutes. Pour the hot chile mixture into the pan, reduce the heat to medium-low, and cook, stirring, until the sauce reaches the simmering point. Do not let the chile scorch. Reduce the heat to low, add salt and pepper to taste, and simmer the sauce gently, still stirring frequently, for about 15 minutes or until it is the consistency you like; then set aside to cool. If the sauce is too thick, thin it out with more beef stock or with water. When cool, pour the sauce into a clean jar, cover tightly, and store it in the refrigerator. The sauce keeps well for up to 2 weeks. To keep it longer, freeze it as soon as it has cooled. Makes about $2^1/_2$ cups.

Red Chile Barbecue Sauce

2 large shallots, chopped
4 cloves garlic, minced
2 Tbs. olive oil
1/2 cup tomato paste
1/4 cup ketchup
1 1/3 cup water
3 Tbs. balsamic vinegar
1/3 cup packed dark brown sugar

4 Tbs. Dijon mustard
1 Tbs. fresh ginger, chopped
1/4 tsp. allspice
1/2 tsp. salt
1 tsp. pepper
1 Tbs. chipotle chile
Pinch cayenne pepper

Sauté shallots and garlic in olive oil in a small saucepan until tender. Add tomato paste, ketchup, and water and blend well. Add all other ingredients. Simmer for 20 minutes, stirring occasionally. Refrigerate. It will keep for one month in a closed container. Makes about 2 cups.

Smoky Barbecue Sauce

This chipotle-flavored hot sauce was developed for slow-cooking beef brisket before a final grilling on the barbecue, but it's a fine mop sauce for pork ribs or chicken, too.

2 Tbs. rendered pork fat
  or bacon drippings
1 large white onion, finely chopped
1 green bell pepper, seeded and
  finely chopped
1 fresh red jalapeño or Fresno chile,
  seeded and minced
2 garlic cloves, minced
2 Tbs. fresh ginger, minced
1 cup catsup
1 cup tomato juice
1/2 cup freshly squeezed orange juice

1/2 cup freshly squeezed lemon juice
1/4 cup apple cider vinegar
2 Tbs. Worcestershire Sauce
2 to 3 Tbs. chipotles en adobo,
  chopped
4 Tbs. turbinado or brown sugar
1 tsp. dry mustard
1/4 tsp. cayenne, or to taste
2 tsp. cumin seed, crushed
2 tsp. coriander seed, crushed
1 tsp. salt

In a large, heavy pot, sauté the onions, green pepper, and chile in hot fat until wilted and browned, about 6 minutes. Toss in the garlic and ginger and sauté another 2 minutes. Stir all the remaining ingredients into the pot and simmer on very low heat for 1 hour. If you like your barbecue sauce thick, continue to simmer until it is reduced to the consistency you like; if you like it thinner, stir in additional fresh orange juice. Makes 3 cups of sauce.

Appetizers

Broiled Oysters Pasilla

1 tsp. chipotle en adobo
1/2 tsp. cumin seed, ground
2 Tbs. olive oil
3 Tbs. pasilla chile puree
  (see page 16)
1 large shallot, minced
3 cloves garlic, minced

1 Tbs. fresh parsley, chopped
1 Tbs. fresh thyme leaves
2 dozen fresh oysters
2 or 3 cups rock salt
1 Tbs. olive oil
1 Tbs. fresh cilantro leaves,
  chopped

In a small bowl, whisk the chipotle, cumin, and 2 tablespoons olive oil into the pasilla chile puree to combine thoroughly. Stir in the minced shallot, garlic, parsley, and thyme. Cover and set aside. Spread a thick layer of coarse salt in a large, shallow baking pan. Scrub the oysters; then shuck and discard the top shells. Arrange oysters on their half-shells on the bed of salt. Spoon the chile mixture over the oysters, dividing it evenly, and drizzle a little olive oil over the chile puree on each oyster. Put the baking pan in the refrigerator and marinate the oysters for 1 hour.

Preheat the oven broiler. Slide the oysters into the broiler 5 to 6 inches from the heat, and broil 3 to 4 minutes until their edges curl and they are hot through. Sprinkle with fresh cilantro and serve immediately. Makes 24 hot appetizers.

Red Chile Honey Baked Brie in Filo Crust

1/2 lb. (approximately) Brie cheese,
  a whole round
1/2 cup butter, melted
1/4 cup red chile honey

8 sheets filo pastry, thawed
1/2 cup shelled pistachio nuts,
  chopped fine

Buy a whole round of Brie, about 4 1/2 to 5 inches in diameter, and slice it in half cross-wise with a sharp knife. Wrap the halves in plastic wrap and keep chilled. In a small, heavy saucepan melt the butter with 2 tablespoons of the red chile honey, stirring to combine. Using a cake pan or other guide, stack the filo sheets and cut them into a 12-inch diameter circle with a sharp knife. You will have 8 circles of pastry; discard the trimmings. Place one circle on a flat surface and, using a pastry brush, coat completely with the melted butter-honey mixture. Working quickly so the pastry sheets do not dry out, cover the first circle with another, and brush with the butter-honey mixture. Continue to repeat layers of pastry, coating each with butter and honey, until you have used all 8 circles of pastry. Immediately place one of the cheese circles on the center of the pastry, cut side up. Sprinkle the pistachio nuts evenly over the cheese, drizzle the nuts with the remaining red chile honey, and place the second circle of cheese over the filling, cut side down. Immediately wrap the filo pastry up over the filled cheese, completely enclosing it in a pastry packet. Wrap tightly with plastic wrap and chill in the refrigerator for at least 1 hour, or until ready to bake.

Remove the wrapped cheese from the refrigerator, place on a buttered baking sheet, seam side down, brush with any remaining butter-honey mixture or with melted butter, and let stand at room temperature for 20 minutes. Preheat the oven to 350 degrees. Bake the cheese for 25 to 35 minutes, or until the pastry is crisp and nicely browned. Let the cheese cool on a rack, and serve barely warm or at room temperature. Makes 16 to 20 appetizer servings.

Chile-Spiced Nuts

Keep chile-coated nuts on hand in the freezer to use in baking, toss into salads, or serve as they are at cocktail parties. Use your favorite kind of nuts or a mixture: peanuts, walnuts, pistachios, cashews, almonds, macadamia nuts, filberts, whatever. Vary the recipe by adding garlic and rosemary for savory nuts, ground chipotle chiles for really hot nuts, or sprinklings of turbinado and ground cinnamon (at the end of the roasting and before the nuts have cooled) for sweeter nuts.

1 tsp. coriander seeds, toasted
1 tsp. cumin seeds, toasted
1/2 tsp. salt
2 tsp. mild red chile powder,
*   or to taste*

1 Tbs. vegetable oil
2 cups nuts

Preheat the oven to 300 degrees. In a mortar or small stone bowl, crush the seeds, salt, and chile powder together to combine thoroughly. In a mixing bowl, sprinkle the oil over the nuts and stir and toss with a spoon to coat the nuts. Sprinkle the chile and spice mixture over the nuts and continue stirring and tossing until the chile is distributed evenly. Pour the nuts into a large baking pan and spread out into a uniform layer. Roast the nuts in the oven for about 15 to 20 minutes, stirring occasionally to turn the nuts and prevent scorching. Don't let the chile and spices scorch, or the nuts will taste bitter! Cool the nuts quickly to room temperature, stirring, then store in airtight containers in the refrigerator, or freeze them. Bring them to room temperature before using. Makes 2 cups.

Chipotle Chicken Empanaditas

The empanaditas can be kept frozen for up to 2 months (before or after baking) and then baked or re-crisped in a hot oven before serving. Pass a bowl of sour cream with the hot empanaditas to cool the fire!

1/4 cup butter, softened
1 1/2 cups cooked chicken breast,
   shredded fine
1 clove garlic, minced
1 dried chipotle chile, washed,
   seeded, soaked, and minced
1 fresh red Fresno or jalapeño chile,
   seeded and minced
2 Tbs. scallion, chopped
1/4 cup each raisins and walnuts,
   chopped

1 large tart apple, peeled and
   finely diced
1/2 lb. thick-sliced bacon, fried,
   drained, and crumbled
Salt and freshly ground pepper,
   to taste
2 lbs. pastry dough, your own
   or from a mix

In a mixing bowl, beat together the softened butter and shredded chicken until well combined. Stir in remaining ingredients (except pastry dough) and mix thoroughly. Butter 2 large baking sheets, and preheat the oven to 425 degrees. Roll out the dough on a lightly floured surface to about 1/8-inch thick. Cut circles from the dough using a 2-inch cookie cutter. Put a spoon of filling on one half of each circle, brush the edges with water and fold into a half-circle, pressing the edges of the pastry together to seal. Crimp the edges with the tines of a fork, set the empanaditas on the baking pans, brush the tops with beaten egg, and bake the pastries for 15 to 20 minutes until they are nicely browned. Serve hot. Makes about 3 dozen empanaditas.

Chipotle Fried Onion Rings

2 large, firm white onions
1/2 cup all-purpose flour
1/4 tsp. salt
1/4 tsp. cumin seeds, ground

Vegetable oil for frying
1 tsp. chipotle powder, or dried
   chipotle chile, ground

Preheat the oven to 250 degrees and line a baking sheet with paper towels. Slice the onions paper thin using a mandolin or a very sharp knife and separate into rings. Heat good vegetable oil (not olive oil) to 375 degrees in a deep fryer, or pour oil 2 to 3 inches deep in a heavy, deep, cast-iron skillet and heat until very hot, but not smoking. In a mixing bowl, whisk the flour, salt, ground cumin and ground chipotle chile together and pour into a heavy-duty plastic freezer bag. Toss the onion rings in the flour mixture, a handful at a time, to coat thoroughly. Shake excess flour from the onion rings and drop them into the hot oil a handful at a time. Stir the onion rings in the hot oil until crisp and golden brown, about 30 to 45 seconds, and remove them to the baking sheet to drain. Sprinkle with additional salt, if desired. Put the baking sheet in the oven and keep warm while you coat and fry the remaining onion rings. Serve immediately. Serves 6 to 10 as an appetizer.

ʃ ʃ ʃ

Chunky Fresh Guacamole

There are many variations of this classic of Mexico and the Southwest, but we don't think you can improve much on this basic recipe. We prefer to use Haas avocados, the ones with the dark, knobby skins.

2 medium ripe avocados
1 Tbs. freshly squeezed lime juice
1/4 tsp. salt
1/8 tsp. Chimayó chile powder
3 scallions, minced
1 fresh red jalapeño chile, minced
1 tsp. fresh oregano leaves, chopped

1 Tbs. fresh cilantro leaves, chopped
1 medium ripe tomato, peeled, seeded, and finely diced
Dash of hot red pepper sauce, if desired

Peel and dice the avocados and put them in a medium bowl. Sprinkle on the lime juice, salt, and chile powder, and crush the avocado with a fork to the desired consistency (we like to leave it pretty chunky). Stir in the scallions, fresh chile, oregano, cilantro, and tomato. Cover the surface with plastic wrap; then set the bowl aside for 30 minutes to develop the flavors. Just before serving, stir the guacamole again and taste for seasoning, adding salt and hot red pepper sauce if desired. Serve with crisp tortilla chips. Makes about 2 cups.

❜ ❜ ❜

Nachos Nuevo Mexico

Flavored with red chile barbecue sauce, these crispy nachos can be served with guacamole, sour cream, and thinly sliced radishes on the side.

2 large white onions,
  sliced very thin
2 Tbs. unsalted butter
Salt and freshly ground pepper,
  to taste
1/2 cup Red Chile Barbecue Sauce
  (see page 30)
1 cup cooked chicken or pork, finely
  shredded

2 cups Monterey Jack cheese,
  shredded
1 tsp. Chimayó chile powder
1 cup well-seasoned, cooked black
  beans, partly crushed
12 small flour tortillas (6 inches
  in diameter) cut in quarters
Vegetable oil for frying tortillas
Coarse salt

Peel the onions and slice very thin, then separate into rings and drop into a large bowl of ice water. Soak the onions for 30 minutes, then drain well and dry with paper towels. In a heavy skillet, melt the butter over medium-low heat, and sauté the onion rings slowly, stirring from time to time, until they are soft and caramelized. Sprinkle the onions with salt and pepper, and set aside. In a small saucepan, mix the Red Chile Barbecue Sauce with the shredded meat and warm over medium heat for about 3 minutes; then set aside. Toss the shredded cheese with the chile powder and set aside. Bring black beans to room temperature before assembling nachos.

In a large, heavy skillet pour fresh vegetable oil to a depth of at least 1 inch. Heat the oil to hot, but not smoking, and fry the tortilla quarters 4 or 5 at a time, turning with tongs, until puffy and golden brown. Drain the tortilla chips on paper towels, and sprinkle with coarse salt. Preheat the oven to 450 degrees. Pick up a tortilla chip, spread it with mashed black beans, top with caramelized onions, shredded meat in sauce, and a sprinkling of shredded cheese. As they are assembled, place the nachos on a baking sheet. Bake the nachos in the hot oven until they are warmed through and the cheese has melted, about 5 minutes. Serve with a favorite salsa on the side. Makes 48 nachos.

Red Chile Olive Quesadillas

Quesadillas can be varied with your favorite fillings or leftover cooked meats and savory vegetables you have on hand. A typical luncheon dish in the Southwest, quesadillas cut into little wedges also make wonderful snacks or appetizers served hot, with salsa, guacamole, or sour cream on the side.

1 medium red onion, thinly sliced
1 Tbs. vegetable oil
Salt and freshly ground pepper, to taste
8 large flour tortillas
1 red bell pepper, roasted, peeled, seeded, and cut in thin strips
1 yellow bell pepper, roasted, peeled, seeded, and cut in thin strips

1 cup Manchego or feta cheese, crumbled
4 fresh Fresno or red jalapeño chiles, seeded and minced
2 cups Monterey Jack cheese, shredded
1/2 to 1 cup brine-cured black olives, seeded and chopped
4 Tbs. fresh cilantro leaves, minced

Preheat the oven to 200 degrees, and line a baking sheet with paper towels. Heat a heavy cast iron skillet and sauté the onion rings in the oil until wilted and just starting to brown, about 8 minutes. Sprinkle the onion rings with salt and pepper and set aside. Wipe out the skillet, leaving a film of oil.

Heat the skillet over a medium-high flame and put 1 tortilla in the skillet. Over 1/2 of the tortilla, distribute 1/8th of the roasted peppers, onion rings, cheeses, chiles, olives, and cilantro (do not mound up the filling, the finished quesadilla should be fairly flat). With a large spatula, fold the other half of the tortilla over the filling (the tortilla will have softened to flexibility by now) and press down gently to hold it in place for about 1 minute. Carefully turn the quesadilla over and continue to cook until the filling is hot and the cheese is melted. Remove the quesadilla to the paper-lined baking sheet and keep warm while you cook the remaining quesadillas. When you are ready to serve, slice each quesadilla into 4 wedges. Makes 32 appetizers.

Red Chile Balsamic Onions

These snappy cocktail onions keep for weeks in the refrigerator and can be served alone or tossed into salads or relishes. If you're short of time try this recipe with canned or frozen pearl onions. The spicy marinade pretty much eliminates the "processed" flavor, but remember that the onions will not be crunchy like fresh ones and will not keep as well.

20 pearl onions
1/2 cup virgin olive oil
2 Tbs. Chimayó chile powder
1 clove garlic, smashed
1 tsp. cumin seeds, toasted
   and slightly crushed

1 pinch sugar
1/3 cup balsamic vinegar
Salt and freshly ground pepper
   to taste

Boil the onions in their skins in a lot of water about 3 or 4 minutes, then drain and rinse briefly in cold water to stop the cooking. When they're cool enough to handle, cut off the tough nub ends and peel the onions very carefully, leaving them intact and beautiful. Whisk together the oil, chile powder, garlic, cumin seed, sugar, vinegar, and salt and pepper. Pour the marinade over the onions in small glass jars, and refrigerate for at least 24 hours and up to 2 weeks. Turn the jars over periodically so all the onions are well marinated. Bring to room temperature before serving. Makes 20 pickled onions.

Red Jalapeños Rellenos

These shrimp-stuffed chiles can also be made with fresh green jalapeño chiles if red ones are unavailable. Preparing these appetizers is much simpler if you purchase red jalapeños in season, then roast and freeze them to have on hand.

20 medium red jalapeño chiles,
    roasted, peeled, and seeded
3 egg whites
2 whole eggs
1/4 tsp. salt
3/4 to 1 cup dark beer

1 cup all-purpose flour
1 lb. medium shrimp (about 20),
    cleaned and deveined
1 lb. cream cheese, softened
20 toothpicks
2 or 3 cups vegetable oil for frying

Roast and peel the jalapeño chiles carefully, leaving the stem intact; make a slit down the side of each chile and gently pull out the seeds. Beat the egg whites until stiff and set aside. Beat the whole eggs and salt with 1/2 cup of the beer until combined. Put the flour in a medium mixing bowl, and beat in the egg mixture slowly until it is combined into a thick batter. Stir in the remaining beer, then gently fold in the beaten egg whites. Chill the batter for 1 hour. Stuff about 1 tablespoon of softened cheese into each chile, then stuff one shrimp into the chile, pulling the sides of the chile together over the body of the shrimp. Pierce the chile through the shrimp with a toothpick to hold it firmly together.

Heat the oil in a deep skillet or a wok. Dip the chiles into the cold batter, let excess batter drain back into the bowl and gently submerge the chiles in the hot oil to cook. Don't crowd the pan. The oil should cook the shrimp to pink and the batter to golden brown in about 2 minutes. Adjust the heat, if necessary. Drain the chiles on the paper towels as they are done. Remove the toothpicks, and serve hot. Makes 20 appetizers.

Red Pork Picadillo

This very Mexican sweet-hot picadillo can be used to stuff chiles or empanadas, or rolled up in small, hot tortillas. If you plan to mince the pork, slice the tenderloin into quarters length-wise, then put it in the freezer until the meat firms up a little for easier mincing. Or have your butcher put the loin through a coarse grinder before you bring it home.

2 garlic cloves, peeled
1 tsp. salt
1 1/2 tsp. Mexican oregano
1/2 tsp. dried sage, crumbled
1 tsp. ground cinnamon
2 tsp. cumin seeds, toasted
1/4 tsp. coriander seeds, toasted
3 black peppercorns
3 whole cloves
1 pork tenderloin (about 3/4 lb.), minced, or coarsely ground
3 Tbs. olive oil

1 medium onion, chopped fine
1 Tbs. ancho chile puree
1 Tbs. pasilla chile puree
1 Tbs. mulato chile puree
1 large ripe tomato, peeled, seeded, and chopped
1/2 cup golden raisins
Salt and freshly ground pepper, to taste
1/3 cup almonds, toasted and chopped fine
2 Tbs. heavy cream

In a mortar or small stone bowl, thoroughly crush the garlic, salt, oregano, sage, cinnamon, cumin and coriander seeds, peppercorns, cloves, and chile powder together. Beat the spice mixture into the minced pork, or mix thoroughly with your hands, to season the meat evenly. In a large, heavy skillet heat the oil over medium-high heat. Add a large spoonful of the pork mixture to the skillet and sauté until just browned, breaking the meat up with a fork, for 2 or 3 minutes; then remove with a slotted spoon to a bowl and reserve. Continue to brown the remaining pork mixture in batches.

In the remaining oil, sauté the onion for 2 minutes. Stir the chile purees into the onions, add the chopped tomato, and cook 3 minutes. Return the browned pork to the skillet, stir in the raisins, and cook the mixture until liquid has evaporated, about 5 minutes. Taste for seasoning, adding salt and freshly ground black pepper as necessary, and stir in the toasted almonds and the cream.

Mound the picadillo on a serving platter and surround with hot, white corn tortillas. Pass your favorite salsa or sour cream on the side. Serves up to 20 guests.

Red-Hot Queso

Keep this rich appetizer dip hot in a chafing dish and serve with fresh tortilla chips or cubes of crusty French bread.

1/2 lb. thick-sliced bacon
1 white onion, finely chopped
2 fresh garlic cloves, minced
1 tsp. cumin seeds, toasted
  and ground
2 large ripe tomatoes, peeled,
  seeded, and finely chopped
2 New Mexico green chiles, roasted,
  peeled, seeded,
  and chopped
2 Tbs. ancho or pasilla chile puree
  (see page 16)
2 tsp. sauce from chipotles en adobo
1 red jalapeño chile, seeded
  and minced

1/2 cup rich chicken stock
1/2 cup whole milk
1 tsp. salt
1 Tbs. unsalted butter
1/2 Tbs. all-purpose flour
Freshly ground black pepper
  to taste
1 cup Monterey Jack cheese,
  finely diced
1 cup mild cheddar cheese,
  finely diced
Dash of liquid hot red pepper sauce,
  to taste

In a large, heavy skillet, cook the bacon until crisp, drain on paper towels, and crumble. Pour all but 1 tablespoon of fat out of the skillet and in it sauté the onion over medium heat until wilted and beginning to brown. Toss in the garlic and ground cumin and sauté 1 minute. Add the chopped tomatoes and green chiles, the chile puree, the adobo sauce, and the minced jalapeño chile to the skillet and sauté, stirring frequently, until thoroughly combined and most of the liquid has evaporated, about 5 minutes. Set aside.

In a small saucepan, bring the stock, milk and salt to a boil. In a medium, heavy saucepan, melt the butter, add the flour, and whisk the roux over medium heat 3 minutes to cook the flour (do not let it brown). Whisk in the boiling liquid, turn the heat to low and simmer the sauce, stirring constantly, about 5 minutes, until thickened. Taste for seasoning, and add salt and freshly ground black pepper. Stir the onion and tomato mixture into the sauce and combine well. Add the diced cheeses and the reserved crumbled bacon to the queso and stir to combine. Taste the queso and add liquid hot red pepper sauce to taste. When the cheese has nearly melted, serve the queso in a chafing dish to keep warm. Serves 12 to 16.

Shrimp Cakes

These little cakes can be sautéed, then frozen on baking sheets and kept in plastic bags up to 2 months for instant appetizers. They are also good made with crab meat or with chopped sea scallops.

2 lbs. shrimp, peeled and deveined
2 Tbs. unsalted butter
2 shallots, minced
1/2 cup scallions, finely chopped
1 fresh red jalapeño chile, seeded
   and minced
1 red bell pepper, seeded
   and finely diced
3/4 cup fresh bread crumbs

2 Tbs. fresh parsley,
   finely chopped
1 large egg, beaten
Salt and freshly ground pepper,
   to taste
Sifted flour for dusting
3 Tbs. olive oil
2 or 3 Tbs. unsalted butter

Finely chop the cleaned shrimp, or pulse in a food processor (but not until mushy). In a heavy skillet, melt the butter and sauté the shallots, scallions, chile, and bell pepper until wilted and soft, about 5 minutes; then transfer to a medium bowl and cool. Stir the shrimp, bread crumbs, parsley, and egg into the vegetable mixture until well combined. Add salt and freshly ground pepper, to taste. Scoop up the mixture by tablespoons and form into balls, then flatten slightly with hands and dust lightly with sifted flour. In a large, nonstick skillet, heat the olive oil and butter until hot. Sauté the cakes in batches until brown, 3 or 4 minutes a side. Keep warm on paper towels in a 200-degree oven until all the cakes are sautéed. Serve hot with Roasted Garlic Chile Mayonnaise (page 23) on the side. Makes 36 to 40 small cakes.

Smoky Chipotle Trout Pâté

The chipotle adds a little smoky heat, without overpowering the delicate flavor of the smoked fish. You can substitute smoked whiting or any other smoked white-fleshed fish for the trout.

2 fillets smoked trout,
  flaked (about 1/4 lb.)
3/4 cup unsalted butter, softened
5 oz. cream cheese, softened
4 oz. mild goat cheese, softened
1 teaspoon chipotle en adobo,
  minced

2 Tbs. freshly squeezed lime juice
1 large scallion, chopped fine
2 Tbs. fresh cilantro, chopped
Salt and freshly ground pepper,
  to taste

Shred the trout meat carefully, removing any fine bones. In a medium mixing bowl, beat the butter with the softened cheeses and chipotle chile until blended well. Beat in the shredded trout and the lime juice (this can be accomplished in a food processor, but we prefer to retain some of the coarser texture of the trout by doing it manually). Stir in the scallion and cilantro, taste for seasoning, and add salt and pepper as necessary. Cover the bowl with plastic wrap and refrigerate for several hours to develop flavors. When ready to serve, bring the pâté to room temperature and mound on a serving platter. Surround with crispy crackers. Makes about 2 dozen appetizers.

Smoky Stewed Garlic

This variation on roasted garlic will keep in the refrigerator for up to 1 week.

1/2 cup rich chicken stock
1/2 cup dry white wine
6 Tbs. dry sherry
5 Tbs. dark soy sauce
6 or 7 large, fresh heads of garlic

1 dried chipotle chile, stemmed
  and seeded
1 teaspoon cumin seeds
5 Tbs. turbinado, raw sugar,
  or dark brown sugar

In a small, heavy, enameled saucepan heat the stock, wines, and soy sauce to a simmer. Separate and peel the garlic cloves, and toss the garlic, the chipotle chile, and the cumin seeds into the simmering liquids. Add the sugar and simmer the mixture, stirring, for 3 minutes. Reduce the heat, cover the pot and stew for 3 hours at a bare simmer. Check the pot from time to time to be certain the liquids have not evaporated, adding more stock by tablespoons to keep the mixture moist. After 3 hours, the garlic cloves will be soft and coated with a rich, dark, sugary glaze. Remove the pot from the heat and let stand another 2 hours, stirring occasionally to keep coating the garlic. Remove the chipotle chile from the pot, pour the garlic into an airtight jar and refrigerate. Bring to room temperature before serving. Serve the glazed cloves whole with toothpicks for spearing; or mash the garlic into a puree for spreading on crackers. Makes about 1 1/2 cups of garlic.

Soups and Stews

Chile Corn Chowder with Shrimp

This corn chowder depends for its distinction on the rich chile flavors in the Spicy Shrimp Broth (page 49). If you haven't any on hand in your freezer, add 1 tablespoon of ancho, mulato, or pasilla chile puree (page 16) to the pot with the chicken broth, and substitute 2 cups of bottled clam juice for the Spicy Shrimp Broth.

2 Tbs. butter
1/2 medium onion, diced fine
1/2 red bell pepper, diced fine
2 cups fresh or frozen corn kernels
2 cups rich chicken broth
2 cups Spicy Shrimp Broth
    (see page 49)

1 cup heavy cream
1/2 lb. cooked shrimp, cut up
1/4 cup parsley, finely chopped
Salt and freshly ground pepper,
    to taste

In a large, heavy pot, melt the butter and sauté the diced onion and red pepper until soft. Stir in the corn kernels and sauté for 5 to 10 minutes. Add the chicken broth and the Spicy Shrimp Broth to the pot and simmer another 10 to 15 minutes. Stir in the cream, the cooked shrimp, and 2 tablespoons parsley, reserving the rest for garnish. Taste for seasoning, adding salt and pepper to taste. Simmer the chowder a few minutes just until heated through (do not overcook the shrimp); and serve immediately in hot soup bowls, sprinkled with a little parsley. Serves 6 to 8.

Pumpkin Soup with Chipotle Chile

For extra zip and crunch, serve this mellow fall soup with Red Chile Ginger Gremolata (see page 22) on the side. It's best to use any variety of sweet little pie pumpkins (2 to 3 pounds each) rather than giant jack-o-lantern pumpkins. They are easier to peel and cube, and the flesh is tender and sweet. Any firm winter squash, such as acorn, or butternut, may be used in place of some or all of the pumpkin; but we do not recommend using canned pumpkin, which will inevitably yield a canned flavor. This soup freezes well in small quantities.

3 lbs. pumpkin
3 Tbs. unsalted butter
3 leeks (white part only),
   finely sliced
2 large shallots, minced
5 scallions, finely sliced
1 garlic clove, minced
2 Tbs. fresh ginger, minced

1 Tbs. pureed chipotle en adobo
8 cups rich chicken stock,
   or 4 of stock and 4 of water
3 Tbs. fresh thyme leaves,
   or 1 Tbs. dried
1 to 2 cups heavy cream, to taste
Salt and freshly ground pepper,
   to taste

Halve the pumpkins, scrape out seeds, peel, and cut into 1-inch cubes with a sharp knife. If the skins are very tough, put the pumpkin halves in a shallow roasting pan, cut side down, with 1/4 cup of water and bake in a 400 degree oven for 20 to 30 minutes, then scrape the pulp out of the shells into a bowl and set aside.

In a large, heavy pot, sauté the leeks, shallots, and scallions in butter for 10 minutes. Add the minced garlic and ginger and the chipotle en adobo and continue cooking for 2 minutes. Stir in the cubed pumpkin, stock, and thyme and simmer 45 minutes or until the pumpkin is very soft. In small batches, puree the soup in a blender or food processor and return to the pot. Add the cream and taste for seasoning, adding salt and freshly ground pepper to taste. Serves 10.

Red Chile Posole

Posole is lime-treated dried corn, called hominy in the South, and is a staple in the pueblos and homes of northern New Mexico. It can be cooked alone and served as a side dish in place of beans or potatoes, or stewed with meats and chiles as a main dish, preferably with a red chile sauce (pages 26 to 29) and sour cream and garnishes on the side. Our recipe uses dried posole, which can be mail ordered if not available locally (page 154). If you must substitute frozen posole, follow the package directions for pre-cooking. Use canned hominy as a last resort, but your finished dish will not have the authentic texture or flavor of New Mexico posole. This robust stew benefits from being made a day ahead, and it freezes well.

2 lbs. fresh pork shoulder,
   cut in 1-inch chunks
1/2 cup each chopped onion,
   carrot, and celery
3 sprigs each fresh parsley
   and oregano
3 garlic cloves
1 bay leaf
6 peppercorns
1 lb. dry posole (about 2 1/2 cups)
4 Tbs. lard or bacon fat
   (or vegetable oil)
2 medium onions, diced

3 or 4 garlic cloves, minced
2 tsp. cumin seeds, toasted
   and ground
1 tsp. each ground cloves
   and dried oregano
4 New Mexico dried red chiles,
   stemmed, seeded, and
   finely crushed
3 tomatoes, peeled, seeded,
   and diced
Salt and freshly ground pepper,
   to taste

Put the pork in a heavy pot with the onion, carrot, celery, parsley, oregano, garlic, bay leaf, and peppercorns and cover with fresh cold water. Bring to a simmer and cook on low heat for 1 1/2 hours, skimming occasionally, then allow the meat to cool in the broth. Drain the pork and set aside, reserving the broth. Wash and drain the dry posole, put it in a large pot, and cover with water by several inches. Bring the posole to a boil, and cook gently for 2 to 3 hours (adding water as necessary to keep the posole covered) until the kernels have softened. Drain the posole thoroughly and set aside.

In a large, heavy pot heat the lard or oil until hot and sauté the diced onion until it is wilted. Toss in the minced garlic and sauté another minute or two. Mix the cumin, cloves, oregano, and crushed chile pods into the onions. Add the tomato, pork, posole, and pork broth and bring the stew to a simmer. Partially cover and simmer on very low heat for 1 to 2 hours, stirring occasionally. Add more water, if necessary, so there's plenty of broth. After the first hour, taste for seasoning and add salt and pepper to taste. Serves 10 to 12.

Spicy Shrimp Broth

This delectable broth makes an elegant first course but also "stretches" as a distinctive enhancement for chowders, soups, and sauces. It is simple, but takes some time and effort to make. We like to prepare it in larger batches and keep it stored in the freezer for instant availability.

1 lb. medium shrimp in shell *3 pasilla chiles*
1 tsp. salt *1 large garlic clove, peeled*
3 guajillo chiles

Wash and peel the shrimp, separately reserving the shells and shrimp debris; devein the shrimp. Bring 4 cups of fresh, cold water and the salt to a rolling boil in a large pot and toss in the cleaned shrimp. When the water returns to the boil (2 or 3 minutes) remove shrimp with a strainer and drop into cold water to stop the cooking, then drain and set aside. Turn the heat under the pot down to simmer and toss in the shells and shrimp debris. Simmer the shells for 15 minutes, remove the pot from the heat, and let the shells cool in the broth.

Meanwhile, wash the chiles and remove the stems, seeds, and veins. Tear the chiles in pieces and put them in a small saucepan with boiling water to cover. Simmer the chiles for about 10 minutes, remove the pan from the heat, and steep the chiles another 10 minutes. Drain the chiles, discarding the water, and put them in a blender with one large, peeled garlic clove and 1 cup of the shrimp cooking water. Blend the mixture until smooth and pour into a saucepan.

In batches, thoroughly blend the cooked shrimp, shells, and remaining broth as smooth as possible, and pour into the pot with the chile mixture. Simmer the mixture over medium heat, stirring frequently, for 10 minutes. Cool the mixture slightly, then press it through a fine sieve lined with a double thickness of cheesecloth rinsed in cold water and wrung dry. Again, you will have to do this procedure in batches, pressing hard on the solids and then lifting the cheesecloth around the mixture and squeezing to extract all the broth. Taste for seasoning and add salt. Makes a little over 2 cups.

J. W. Hansel's Chile Con Carne

Tucson chile afficionado J. W. Hansel perfected this robust chile over a period of years. The beans are optional, but they will help to cut the heat if the pequin chiles are too hot for you. Lots of crumbly, hot cornbread is an essential! This chile is even better the next day.

1 lb. dried black beans
1/4 lb. fresh, unsalted, unsmoked
   lean bacon (pork belly)
1/2 lb. veal shank
1/2 medium white onion, sliced
Herb bouquet
2 tsp. dried epazote (optional)
1 Tbs. salt
3 to 4 Tbs. lard or bacon grease
3 lbs. beef brisket, cut into
   1 by 1-inch chunks
1 medium onion, chopped
1 large green bell pepper, chopped

3 cloves garlic, chopped
4 Tbs. Santa Cruz or other
   red chile powder
2 tsp. crushed pequin chile
3 Tbs. ground cumin
2 oz. lemon juice
2 Tbs. vinegar
2 28-oz. cans peeled tomatoes
1 28-oz. can tomato sauce
1 10-oz. can beef broth
Salt and freshly ground pepper,
   to taste

Soak the dried black beans overnight in water to cover in a large pot; drain and discard water. In a large, heavy pot, cover the beans with water; add bacon, onion, and herb bouquet (2 sprigs parsley, 2 unpeeled garlic cloves, 1 large bay leaf, 1 clove, 2 sprigs fresh thyme tied in cheesecloth). Bring to a simmer and cook uncovered until done, from 2 to 4 hours depending on the beans. Thirty minutes before the end of cooking time, add 2 teaspoons of dried epazote and the salt. When the beans are cooked, discard the herb bouquet; remove the bacon, cut up the meat, and set it aside. Leave beans in their cooking liquid.

In a heavy chile pot (8 quarts or so), brown the beef chunks in hot bacon grease a handful at a time, remove the chunks from the pot and set aside. Pour off all but a little of the fat, and in it sauté the chopped onion and green pepper until soft. Add the garlic, chiles, cumin, lemon juice, vinegar, tomatoes, tomato sauce, and beef broth. Return the beef to the pot, stir and bring to a boil. Reduce heat and simmer, uncovered, about 2 or 3 hours, stirring periodically. Add more beef broth or bean-cooking liquid as needed to keep the chile moist. Taste for seasoning, and add salt and pepper, and more pequin chile to taste. Drain the beans, reserving liquid, and add to the pot. Simmer the chile another 30 minutes, adding more bean-cooking liquid as necessary. Serve with grated cheese, sour cream, or whatever condiments you like, hot cornbread on the side. Serves 10 to 12.

New Mexico Tortilla Soup

There are many variations on basic tortilla soup, which begins with whatever rich meat or vegetable broth is on hand, a handful of ground red chiles, and yesterday's tortillas. These additions can be varied—you may come up with others you prefer.

1/2 cup vegetable oil for frying
6 white corn tortillas
1 large white onion, diced
2 cloves garlic, minced
1/3 to 1/2 cup Chimayó chile powder
1 1/2 tsp. cumin seed, toasted and ground
1 tsp. Mexican oregano
7 cups rich chicken stock
2 cups fresh or frozen corn kernels, cooked
1 cup cooked black beans, rinsed and drained

2 large tomatoes, peeled, seeded, and diced
Salt and freshly ground pepper, to taste
1 cup cooked chicken meat, chopped
2 ripe avocados, peeled and sliced
1 cup Monterey Jack cheese, shredded
3 Tbs. cilantro leaves, chopped
1 large lime, cut into 6 wedges

Pour 1/2 cup vegetable oil in a deep, heavy pot and heat until hot but not smoking. Cut the tortillas in strips 1/4 inch to 1/2 inch wide and fry in the hot oil until golden and crisp, sprinkle with salt and set aside to drain (or just use your favorite packaged tortilla chips if you don't have corn tortillas on hand). Pour all but 2 tablespoons of the oil out of the pot, reduce the heat to medium and add the diced onion. Sauté the onion slowly until it is translucent and just beginning to color (about 5 to 10 minutes). Stir the minced garlic into the onions and continue to sauté another two minutes. Sprinkle the chile powder, cumin, and oregano into the onions and cook, stirring constantly, for another 2 minutes. Slowly pour in the chicken stock, mixing thoroughly, bring to a simmer and cook 5 minutes. Add the corn, beans, and tomatoes and simmer another 10 minutes. Taste the soup for seasoning and add salt and pepper to taste. Add the cooked chicken and simmer for another 5 minutes. To serve, distribute the crisp tortilla strips and some slices of avocado among 6 soup bowls; ladle the soup on top; sprinkle each serving with shredded cheese and chopped cilantro; and serve a lime wedge on the side. Serves 6.

Red Chile Beef Stew

A rich and peppery beef stew with just a sweet note of New Mexico red chiles, this dish is spectacular served over creamy, garlic mashed potatoes.

3/4 cup good olive oil
1 Tbs. freshly ground pepper
3 lbs. beef brisket, cut in
    2-inch pieces
4 Tbs. good olive oil
2 cups dry red wine
1/4 lb. fresh, unsalted, lean bacon
    (pork belly), finely diced

3 large onions, diced
6 cloves garlic, minced
4 Tbs. Chimayó red chile powder
2 cups Roma tomatoes, peeled
    and crushed
1 cup beef stock
Salt and freshly ground pepper,
    to taste

Mix 3/4 cup olive oil with the black pepper in a glass bowl, add the beef, mix to coat, and marinate in the refrigerator overnight, covered. Heat 3 tablespoons olive oil in a large, heavy skillet and brown the beef in batches, adding oil as necessary. Transfer the beef to a stewing casserole. Deglaze the browning pot with the red wine and pour over the beef. Add a tablespoon of olive oil to the skillet and sauté the fresh bacon over low to medium heat for 15 minutes. Add the onions to the skillet and cook until soft and the bacon is cooked through. Add the garlic and sauté 2 minutes. Sprinkle the chile powder over the onion mixture and stir for 1 minute. Scrape the onion mixture into the casserole. Add the crushed tomatoes and the stock to the casserole. Bring the stew to a boil, reduce heat, and simmer about 2 hours. After the meat is tender, boil the stew 15 or 20 minutes to reduce and thicken the sauce.

Roasted Pepper and Corn Soup

This soup is wonderful to start a seafood meal, or served on its own with tortilla chips and a salad. It keeps well for several days in the refrigerator.

1 dried New Mexico red chile,
  or more to taste
1 medium onion, diced
3 Tbs. olive oil
3 garlic cloves, minced
1 Tbs. fresh ginger, minced
5 red bell peppers, roasted,
  peeled, and seeded
1 1/2 tsp. cumin seed, toasted
  and ground

1 tsp. Mexican oregano
4 cups rich chicken stock
2 cups cream
2 cups fresh or frozen corn kernels
Salt and freshly ground pepper,
  to taste
2 scallions, sliced thin

Wipe the red chile with a damp cloth, remove stem and seeds, tear in pieces and cover with a small amount of boiling water. Leave to soak about 20 minutes. In a large saucepan, sauté the onion in the olive oil until soft. Add the garlic, and ginger and sauté for 1 minute, then set aside. Coarsely chop the roasted bell peppers and put into a blender jar; add the onions, garlic and ginger, the cumin and oregano, and the softened red chile with a few tablespoons of the soaking water. Blend to a smooth puree, adding a little of the chicken stock as necessary to keep the mixture circulating. Pour the puree into the saucepan and whisk in the remaining chicken stock, combining thoroughly. Bring to a simmer and add up to 2 cups of cream, to your taste, and the corn kernels. Gently heat the soup through (do not allow to boil) and taste carefully for seasoning, adding salt and pepper to taste. Serve with a sprinkle of sliced scallion on top. Serves 6 to 8.

Tomato Chile Soup

This soup is good hot or at room temperature served with a dollop of sour cream and a sprinkling of chives. It freezes well. The quality of the soup will depend not only on the quality of the fresh tomatoes you can obtain locally, but on the quality and freshness of your chicken or vegetable broth. If possible, make up your broth at home with the best ingredients you can buy.

1 medium onion, chopped
1 stalk celery, chopped
$^1/_2$ Tbs. extra virgin olive oil
1 potato, peeled and chopped
3 garlic cloves, minced
4 large ripe tomatoes, peeled,
   seeded, and chopped

1 Tbs. chopped fresh oregano
4 cups rich chicken stock
   or vegetable broth
2 or 3 Tbs. ancho or pasilla puree
   (see page 16)
$^1/_2$ cup sun-dried tomatoes

In a large, heavy soup pot sauté the onion and celery in the olive oil until soft. Add the potato, garlic, tomatoes, and oregano and sauté another 10 minutes. Stir some of the broth into the chile puree to thin it out, then mix the puree into the broth and add the broth to the pot. Bring to a boil, lower the heat, and simmer the soup for 20 minutes. Cool the soup slightly and puree in a blender, in batches. Return the soup to the pot and add the sun-dried tomatoes. Heat through and serve with a dollop of sour cream and a sprinkling of fresh chopped chives on top. Serves 8 to 10.

Veracruz Chowder

You may substitute other local, fresh seafood for the shrimp, snapper, and scallops. If you don't have any Spicy Shrimp Broth (page 49) on hand, use bottled clam juice simmered with 2 or 3 tablespoons of ancho or pasilla chile puree, preferably a combination of the two.

12 large shrimp, peeled
  and cleaned
1 1/2 lbs. red snapper fillet,
  cut in 1-inch cubes
1 lb. sea scallops, cut in half
4 garlic cloves, minced
3 Tbs. extra virgin olive oil
2 large onions, chopped
3 Tbs. olive oil
2 Tbs. all-purpose flour
2 Tbs. tomato paste

2 cups bottled clam juice
2 cups Spicy Shrimp Broth
  (see page 49)
3 large tomatoes, peeled,
  seeded, and diced
1/2 tsp. Mexican oregano
1/2 to 1 tsp. chile Caribe, to taste
2 fresh poblano chiles, roasted,
  peeled, seeded, and cut in strips
3 Tbs. minced fresh cilantro

In a medium bowl, toss the shrimp, snapper fillet, and scallops with minced garlic and olive oil and set aside. In a large pot, cook the chopped onion in oil until soft. Stir in the flour and the tomato paste and cook, whisking, for 3 minutes. Slowly pour the clam juice and the Spicy Shrimp Broth into the pot, whisking, and simmer until slightly thickened. Stir in the tomatoes, oregano, and chile Caribe and simmer 10 minutes. Add the shrimp, snapper and scallops to the pot and simmer 5 minutes, or until fish is cooked through. Stir in the poblano strips and cilantro. Serves 8 to 10.

Salads

Jícama, Apple, and Asiago Slaw
with Ancho Chile Mayonnaise

SLAW

1 medium jícama
1 large Granny Smith apple

¹/₂ lb. Asiago cheese

DRESSING

1 Tbs. freshly squeezed lime juice
¹/₃ to ¹/₂ cup mayonnaise
1 Tbs. spicy brown mustard
1 Tbs. honey

¹/₂ tsp. salt
1 Tbs. ancho chile puree
   (see page 16)

Peel the jícama and apple and slice into matchsticks. Slice the cheese into matchsticks and mix with the jícama and apple in a medium bowl. Mix the dressing ingredients and pour over the slaw. Add salt and pepper to taste. Chill for one hour, or up to 24 hours. Add additional chile puree to taste before serving. Serves 6.

Citrus and Scallion Salad
with Chile-Glazed Piñon Nuts

In summer, include a good selection of field greens and savory lettuces from the local farmer's market.

SALAD

2 large oranges
1 large grapefruit
1 lb. mixed lettuces and
   field greens

4 scallions, sliced
¹/₄ cup Chile-Spiced Nuts
   (piñons) (page 33)

DRESSING

¹/₂ cup light olive oil
4 Tbs. red wine vinegar
2 to 3 tsp. sugar, to taste

¹/₄ tsp. salt
2 tsp. red chile pepper sauce,
   or to taste

Section the citrus fruits carefully, removing all pith and seeds, and drain thoroughly (so as not to dilute the dressing). Mix lettuces, citrus, scallions, and nuts in a large bowl. Whisk dressing ingredients together, pour over salad, and toss lightly to mix. Serves 6 to 8.

Spinach Salad with Sautéed Feta, Wild Mushrooms, and Pasilla Chile Dressing

This elegant warm salad takes some last-minute attention but is worth the effort. If wild mushrooms are not available in your area, use a mix of whatever fresh mushrooms your local groceries carry.

DRESSING

1 dried pasilla chile
1 clove garlic
4 Tbs. red wine vinegar

2 Tbs. virgin olive oil
1/3 cup virgin olive oil

SALAD

1 lb. wild mushrooms (or a mix
   of domestic mushrooms)
1 Tbs. olive oil

1/2 lemon, juiced
1/2 tsp. salt
freshly cracked pepper, to taste

6 to 10 oz. good feta cheese,
   cut in 1-inch cubes
1 large egg, beaten
1 cup crispy Panko or dry bread
   crumbs

3 Tbs. olive oil
2 bunches fresh spinach,
   washed, trimmed, and dried
1 small red onion or several shallots,
   very thinly sliced

Wash, stem, and seed the pasilla chile. Break it into a one-cup measure and pour just enough boiling water over the pieces to cover them; let the chile soak 5 to 10 minutes until soft. Drain the chile pieces and put them in a blender with the garlic clove, vinegar, and 2 tablespoons of virgin olive oil. Set blender on high speed to puree and set aside.

Clean, trim, and chop the mushrooms. In a large skillet heat 1 tablespoon olive oil over a high flame until hot. Add the mushrooms, lemon juice, salt, and pepper and sauté, stirring, over high heat until the mushrooms have released all their liquids and are browned and nearly dry. Set the mushrooms aside and keep warm. Dip the feta cubes in the beaten egg and roll in Panko or dry bread crumbs to coat thoroughly. Heat 3 tablespoons of olive oil in the skillet over medium flame. Sauté the feta cubes, turning, until they are golden brown. Remove the cubes to paper towels to drain.

Just before serving, toss the spinach, red onion, and mushrooms together in a large bowl. Heat 1/3 cup virgin olive oil gently in a small pan until nearly hot, and whisk into the pasilla dressing. Pour the warm dressing over the salad and mix gently (the spinach will wilt a little), then distribute the salad among serving plates and top with feta cubes. Serves 6.

Roasted Winter Vegetable Salad
with Red Chile Vinaigrette

Serve this hearty, cold-weather salad barely warm as an accompaniment for roasted poultry or game. You can use your favorite combinations of roasting vegetables and herbs. Carrots and beets work especially well with the Chimayó chile dressing.

SALAD

8 small beets
8 small carrots
6 small parsnips
12 tiny red potatoes (about the size of boiling onions)
12 small boiling onions
3 Tbs. good olive oil

Salt and freshly ground pepper, to taste
2 garlic cloves
3 sprigs each of fresh oregano and parsley (optional)
1 lb. mixed greens

VINAIGRETTE

4 Tbs. red wine vinegar
2 Tbs. fresh parsley leaves, minced
4 tsp. fresh thyme leaves, minced
1 tsp. Chimayó or other red chile powder, to taste

1/2 cup virgin olive oil (or less, to taste)
Salt and freshly cracked black pepper, to taste

Preheat the oven to 400 degrees. Scrub the beets, carrots, parsnips, and potatoes with a vegetable brush and pat them dry. Cut the beets, carrots, and parsnips into chunks about the same size as the boiling onions. Leave the tiny potatoes whole with their skins on. Drop the onions into boiling water for 15 seconds and slip off their skins. Scatter the vegetables and garlic into a large glass baking dish, sprinkle with the olive oil, salt, and pepper and toss to coat. Tie the parsley and oregano sprigs together with a piece of kitchen string, and toss the bundle on top of the vegetables. Cover the pan with foil and roast for 30 minutes. Lift the foil and gently toss the vegetables. Continue roasting another 15 minutes. Remove the foil and the herb sprigs from the pan, and roast uncovered until the vegetables are browned and cooked through, about 15 more minutes.

Whisk the dressing ingredients together, adding the olive oil in a slow stream until the mixture is emulsified, and taste for seasoning. Remove the garlic cloves from the pan and pour the dressing over the vegetables, tossing gently. Let the salad rest in the pan until the vegetables are cooled to barely warm, about an hour. Put a handful of mixed greens on each of 6 to 8 salad plates, and divide the salad among the plates. Serves 8.

Southwest Potato Salad

This potato salad combines Mediterranean flavors with the snap of hot chiles and the distinctive southwestern savor of fresh cilantro. If keeping the salad cool on the way to a picnic is a problem, substitute an olive oil vinaigrette for the mayonnaise and cut the lime juice to 1 teaspoon.

SALAD

2 lbs. new potatoes
$3/4$ cup brine-cured black olives, sliced
$3/4$ cup sun-dried tomatoes packed in oil, drained and sliced
$1/2$ cup chopped scallions

$1/4$ cup red bell pepper, minced
$1/2$ fresh red jalapeño or Fresno chile, seeded and minced
$1/2$ cup fresh cilantro leaves, chopped

DRESSING

$2/3$ cup mayonnaise
2 tsp. freshly squeezed lime juice
1 tsp. Chimayó or other red chile powder, or to taste
$1/2$ tsp. cumin seed, toasted and ground

$1/2$ tsp. pressed garlic (optional)
Salt and freshly cracked black pepper, to taste

Scrub the new potatoes and cook in salted, boiling water until done (15 or 20 minutes). Drain and cool the potatoes, then cut into bite-sized chunks. Gently mix the olives, tomatoes, scallions, bell pepper, red chile, and cilantro into the potatoes. Whisk the dressing ingredients together and taste for seasoning. Mix the dressing into the vegetables and refrigerate for several hours to let the flavors meld. Serves 6 to 8.

Chile Caribe Chicken Salad

A tropical main-course salad for a summer supper, with creamy mango and crunchy cubes of water chestnut to complement the savory chicken and cool greens.

DRESSING

1/3 cup light olive oil
2 Tbs. freshly squeezed lime juice
2 Tbs. honey
2 Tbs. coarsely ground
    or dijon mustard

1 large clove garlic, minced
1 tsp. Chimayó chile powder

SALAD

4 skinless, boneless chicken breast
    halves
4 tsp. Chile Caribe Rub (page 20)
2 fresh mangoes, peeled and sliced

1/2 cup water chestnuts, diced
1 lb. mixed salad greens
    (about 4 handfuls)
Zest of one fresh lime

Whisk dressing ingredients in a small bowl, add the diced water chestnuts and set aside. Peel and slice the mangoes and set aside. Arrange fresh greens on four large plates. Sprinkle each chicken breast half with Chile Caribe Rub (1/2 teaspoon each side) and spread evenly over the meat. Sauté the chicken breasts in hot oil until browned and just cooked through (about 5 to 7 minutes per side, do not overcook!). Remove the breasts to a cutting board and cut into thin slices on the bias. Arrange the mango slices and warm chicken on the greens and drizzle with dressing. Sprinkle the salads with fresh lime zest. Serves 4.

Serious Southwestern Slaw

SLAW

1/2 green cabbage, finely shredded
1/2 purple cabbage,
    finely shredded
1 red bell pepper, cut into
    fine matchsticks
1 yellow bell pepper, cut into
    fine matchsticks

1 green bell pepper, cut into
    fine matchsticks
1 red jalapeno or Fresno chile,
    seeded and minced
3 scallions, sliced thin

DRESSING

³/4 cup mayonnaise

¹/2 cup sour cream

1 Tbs. honey

2 Tbs. cider vinegar

1 tsp. red chile powder

Whisk the mayonnaise, sour cream, honey, vinegar, and chile powder together in a small bowl and let stand while you prepare the slaw. Toss the vegetables together in a large salad bowl, pour the dressing over the vegetables, and mix well. Serves 6.

Gingered Chile Slaw

This hearty slaw is an adaptation of New York's Union Square Cafe version of a traditional Burmese slaw. Serve with grilled fish or fowl or on its own as a vegetarian main dish.

SLAW

¹/2 cabbage, thinly sliced
   (about 4 or 5 cups)

1 large poblano chile, roasted,
   peeled, and cut in julienne strips

1 large yellow bell pepper,
   cut in julienne strips

1 large red bell pepper,
   cut in julienne strips

2 scallions, sliced fine

¹/4 cup fresh cilantro, chopped

2 Tbs. Chile-Spiced Nuts
   (peanuts), chopped (page 33)

1 Tbs. sesame seeds, toasted

2 tsp. coarse salt

¹/8 tsp. freshly ground black pepper

DRESSING

1¹/2 Tbs. minced fresh ginger

1 Tbs. minced fresh red jalapeño or
   Fresno chile

2 tsp. minced garlic

¹/4 cup freshly squeezed lime juice

¹/4 cup minced shallots

1 Tbs. dark soy sauce

1 Tbs. honey

1 Tbs. dark sesame oil

¹/2 cup peanut oil

Mix the vegetables, peanuts, sesame seeds, salt, and pepper in a large bowl. Whisk dressing ingredients together and let stand up to an hour. Pour the dressing over the slaw and combine thoroughly. Chill the slaw for an hour or up to 24 hours. Serves 6 to 8.

Roasted Beef and Field Greens
with Red Chile Vinaigrette

An elegant way to make use of leftover roast, this recipe can also be made with roasted leg of lamb. The meat should be roasted to rare or medium rare, still quite pink and tender. Use an interesting variety of lettuces with some savory additions, such as chicory, arugula, and wild greens if they are available.

SALAD

2 cups good roasted beef
   (about a lb.)

1 small red onion
6 cups mixed field greens

DRESSING

4 Tbs. red wine vinegar
2 Tbs. fresh parsley leaves, minced
4 tsp. fresh thyme leaves, minced
1 tsp. Chimayó or other red chile
   powder, or to taste

$^1/_2$ cup virgin olive oil (or less,
   to taste)
Salt and freshly cracked black
   pepper, to taste

Wash, dry, and chill the field greens. Slice the red onion into thin rounds, separate the rings, and soak them in cold water for 10 or 15 minutes. Carefully trim all fat and gristle from the beef and slice it thin, then into manageable strips (about 1 inch by 2 inches). Whisk the dressing ingredients together, adding the olive oil in a slow stream until the mixture is emulsified, and taste for seasoning. Pour the dressing over the beef strips in a glass or ceramic bowl. Drain and dry the onion rings and mix gently into the beef and dressing. Let the beef and onions stand in the dressing at room temperature for at least half an hour so the flavors will meld. Just before serving, toss the beef, onions, and dressing with the chilled field greens, and divide the salad among individual plates. Serves 4 to 6.

Fresh Fruit Salad with
Spicy Avocado Dressing

The avocado dressing also goes well with cold chicken or turkey; and, if you omit the honey and add half a minced garlic clove, it partners beautifully with cold shrimp or scallops, or with a bowl of summer vegetables.

SALAD

1 large mango
3 apricots, peeled and quartered
3 plums, peeled and quartered
2 cups strawberries, halved

1 small bunch green grapes, washed and stemmed
1 lb. mixed lettuces

DRESSING

$1/2$ medium avocado, peeled and mashed
$1/2$ cup plain yogurt
1 Tbs. honey, or to taste
2 scallions, minced (white part only)
$1/2$ tsp. lemon zest

$1/4$ tsp. orange zest
$1/8$ tsp. salt
$1/4$ tsp. ground cumin
$1/8$ tsp. freshly ground black pepper
$1/2$ tsp. minced Fresno or red jalapeno chile
2 Tbs. light cream, or to taste

Whisk the dressing ingredients together in a medium bowl, or mix in a blender if you prefer. Adjust seasoning to taste, and drizzle over mixed fresh fruits and greens. Serves 6 to 8.

Southwest Salad
with Red Chile Blue Cheese Dressing

This version of the popular salad is rich, filling, and piquant with flavor—a robust luncheon or supper dish that can be served at any time of year.

SALAD

1 lb. mixed leaf lettuce greens, torn
1 ripe avocado, pitted and diced
1/2 cup cooked corn kernels, drained
1/2 cup cooked black beans, drained
1/2 cup jícama, peeled and cut
   into matchsticks
1/2 cup zucchini, cut into
   matchsticks

1/2 cup red bell pepper, cut
   into matchsticks
1/4 cup brine-cured black olives,
   pitted and sliced
2 scallions, sliced
1 fresh serrano chile, seeded
   and minced

DRESSING

1 cup mayonnaise
2 to 3 Tbs. white wine
2 Tbs. light cream
1/8 tsp. freshly ground black pepper

1 small clove garlic, minced
1/2 tsp. Chimayó or other
   red chile powder
1/4 cup blue cheese, crumbled

Whisk dressing ingredients together in a small bowl and let stand for at least 30 minutes. Toss salad ingredients together in a large bowl, pour dressing over salad, and mix gently. Serves 6.

Vegetables

Twice-Baked Red Jalapeño Potatoes

The potatoes may be prepared up to 2 hours ahead and reheated for serving.

8 large russet potatoes,
  scrubbed and oiled
3 cups gorgonzola or other
  blue cheese, crumbled
4 oz. cream cheese, softened
1 Tbs. Chimayó chile powder
1/2 to 3/4 cups light cream, scalded
Salt and freshly ground pepper,
  to taste

4 scallions, finely minced
2 large red jalapeño chiles,
  seeded and finely minced
1/2 cup freshly grated Parmesan
  cheese
2 Tbs. fresh chives, chopped

Preheat the oven to 400 degrees. Pierce the potatoes several times with a metal skewer, and bake on a rack set at the middle third of the oven for about 1 hour, or until the potatoes are cooked through. Cool the potatoes about 5 minutes. Cleanly slice the top third off each potato and gently scoop the meat out of the bottoms into a large bowl, leaving a 1/4-inch thick shell. Mash the potatoes coarsely, add the blue cheese, cream cheese, chile powder, and 1/2 cup of the cream, and mix thoroughly to desired consistency, adding cream by tablespoons as necessary. Do not over-mix or add too much cream, or you will end up with a creamy puree that has no character. Taste for seasoning and add salt and pepper to taste. Stir the scallions and minced jalapeño chiles into the potato mixture; then divide the mixture among the 8 potato shells, mounding it gently. Sprinkle the grated Parmesan cheese over the potatoes, place them on a baking sheet and return to the oven at 400 degrees until the potatoes are heated through and the tops are browned, about 15 minutes. Sprinkle the potatoes with chopped chives. Serves 8.

Baked Red Chile Sweet Yams

1/4 cup freshly squeezed
    orange juice
1/4 cup red chile honey
6 medium sweet potatoes or yams,
    scrubbed, cooked, and peeled
Salt and freshly ground pepper,
    to taste

1/2 cup dark brown sugar
1 cup Chile-Spiced Nuts (pecans),
    coarsely chopped (page 33)
1 Tbs. grated orange zest
4 Tbs. unsalted butter,
    cut into small dice
1 Tbs. fresh sage leaves, minced

Preheat the oven to 375 degrees. Butter a 2-quart casserole or glass baking dish with high sides. In a small, heavy saucepan stir the orange juice into the red chile honey over a low flame, just until the honey is dissolved in the juice. Slice the cooled sweet potatoes in rounds about 1/4-inch thick, and put a layer of slices in the bottom of the casserole, overlapping slightly. Sprinkle the layer lightly with salt and pepper to taste, brown sugar, chopped pecans and orange zest. Drizzle some of the honey mixture over the top, and dot with pieces of butter. In the same manner, continue layers of potatoes and seasonings until the casserole is filled. Bake the casserole, uncovered, 30 to 40 minutes until the potatoes are glazed and heated through. Sprinkle the casserole with minced fresh sage. Serves 8 to 10.

Skillet Butternut Squash
with Cilantro-Mint Salsa

Any firm winter squash or thin slices of sweet baking pumpkin would do well for this recipe. We have also used sliced Japanese eggplant and sliced green tomatoes. You can omit the light corn meal crust if you prefer, and simply sauté or grill the vegetables.

1 large butternut squash,
  about 3 lbs.
1/2 cup milk
1/2 cup corn meal
1/4 tsp. salt
Freshly ground pepper,
  to taste

1 to 3 Tbs. olive oil, for frying
Salt and freshly ground pepper,
  to taste
1 cup Cilantro Mint Salsa
  (page 24)

Preheat the oven to 250 degrees. Cut the narrow neck from the squash. Peel the squash and slice in 1/4-inch-thick rounds. Dip the rounds in milk, then shake in a bag with the corn meal, salt, and pepper to lightly coat. Heat the olive oil in a large, heavy skillet and sauté the squash over high heat in batches, turning once, until lightly browned, about 5 to 8 minutes. Drain the squash slices on paper towels, season with salt and pepper and keep warm in the oven, uncovered, until all the squash has been cooked. Transfer the squash to a platter, drizzle with Cilantro Mint Salsa and serve remaining Salsa separately. Serves 4 to 6.

Chile Scalloped Potatoes
with Asiago and Sage

This dish can be put together a day ahead of time and baked just before serving.

2 Tbs. unsalted butter
2 medium onions, sliced thin
2 cloves garlic, minced
1¹/₂ Tbs. Chimayó chile powder
¹/₄ tsp. nutmeg, freshly grated
¹/₄ tsp. cumin seeds, toasted
    and ground
2 Tbs. fresh sage, chopped fine
2¹/₂ lbs. potatoes, peeled
    and sliced thin

1 cup dry bread crumbs
1 cup Asiago or other mild
    white cheese, grated
1 Tbs. fresh sage, chopped fine
¹/₄ tsp. salt
¹/₈ tsp. freshly ground pepper
2 Tbs. virgin olive oil
1¹/₂ cups light cream

Preheat the oven to 400 degrees. Melt the butter in a large, heavy pot and sauté the sliced onions until they are soft and translucent, 7 or 8 minutes. Add the garlic, chile powder, nutmeg, and cumin and sauté another 1 or 2 minutes; then remove from heat and mix in 2 tablespoons of sage and the sliced potatoes. In a medium bowl, toss together the bread crumbs, grated cheese, 1 tablespoon of sage, salt, pepper, and olive oil. Butter a glass or pottery casserole and layer half the potato and onion mixture on the bottom; cover with half of the cheese mixture; layer the remaining potato and onion mixture over the crumbs; gently pour the cream over the potatoes; then sprinkle the remaining cheese mixture over the top of the casserole. Dot the cheese mixture with butter, and bake the casserole about 1 hour until the potatoes are tender and the cheese topping is golden brown. Serves 8.

Creamy Red Chile Posole

Posole is lime-treated dried corn, called hominy in the South, and is a staple in the pueblos and homes of northern New Mexico. This casserole has more in common with southern hominy dishes than with southwestern posole stew (see Red Chile Posole, page 48). Posole can be mail ordered from many of the chile sources we have listed on pages 154 and 155. If you substitute frozen posole, follow the package directions for pre-cooking. Canned hominy requires no pre-cooking.

1 lb. of posole (about 2^1/$_2$ cups dry,
  5 cups cooked)
2 Tbs. unsalted butter
1 medium onion, diced
1 red bell pepper, seeded and diced
2 cloves garlic, minced
1 Tbs. Chimayó chile powder
^{1}/$_2$ cup rich chicken or vegetable
  stock
1 tsp. Mexican oregano
^{1}/$_2$ tsp. fresh thyme leaves, chopped

^{1}/$_2$ tsp. salt
Freshly ground pepper, to taste
^{3}/$_4$ cup heavy cream
^{1}/$_2$ cup Monterey Jack cheese,
  shredded
^{1}/$_2$ cup plus 2 Tbs. cilantro leaves,
  chopped
^{1}/$_4$ cup mild cheddar cheese,
  shredded
2 Tbs. cilantro leaves, chopped

Wash and drain the dry posole, put it in a large pot and cover with water by several inches. Bring the posole to a boil, and simmer gently for 2 or 3 hours (adding water as necessary to keep the posole covered) until the kernels have softened. Drain the posole thoroughly and set aside.

Preheat the oven to 375 degrees, and butter a large glass baking dish or casserole. Melt the butter in a large, heavy skillet and sauté the diced onion and pepper until soft, about 8 minutes. Add the garlic and sauté 3 minutes more. Sprinkle the chile powder over the vegetables, then mix in the drained posole. Add the stock, oregano, thyme, salt, and a few grindings of black pepper and simmer the mixture for 5 minutes. Stir in the cream, remove the skillet from the flame, and stir in the shredded cheeses and ^{1}/$_2$ cup chopped cilantro. Pour the mixture into the prepared casserole, cover and bake 20 to 30 minutes until sauce is thickened and bubbly. Remove the cover from the casserole and sprinkle the top with the shredded cheddar. Set the casserole under the broiler until the cheddar is melted and beginning to brown. Let the casserole sit 5 minutes, sprinkle with the remaining cilantro, and serve. Serves 8 to 10.

Red Chile Carrots Cointreau

1 lb. fresh young carrots, peeled and cut in 2-inch julienne strips
3 Tbs. unsalted butter
1 tsp. Chimayó chile powder
1 tsp. grated orange rind

2 Tbs. Cointreau or other orange liqueur, or to taste
Salt and freshly cracked black pepper
1 to 2 Tbs. fresh parsley, minced

Steam the julienned carrots over boiling water 3 to 5 minutes until barely crisp-tender (do not overcook). Melt butter in a heavy, nonstick sauté pan; add carrots and toss to coat. Sprinkle carrots with chile powder, grated orange rind, and salt and cracked pepper to taste. Sauté over medium high heat about 2 minutes. Pour in Cointreau or other orange liqueur and continue to sauté until liquid has evaporated and carrots are nicely glazed, about 3 minutes. Sprinkle with parsley and serve. Serves 4.

Chile-Roasted Cauliflower

Slow roasting permits the vegetable to absorb the chile flavor gradually and turn a lovely golden brown color. Try this treatment for parsnips, turnips, broccoli, and carrots.

1 large head cauliflower
2 or 3 garlic cloves, minced
1 Tbs. Chimayó red chile powder, to taste
1/2 tsp. dried New Mexico red chile, crushed

1 tsp. cumin seeds, toasted and ground
Salt to taste
4 Tbs. good olive oil
1/4 cup cilantro leaves, chopped
1/2 lime, juiced

Heat the oven to 325 degrees. Separate the florets from the cauliflower and toss in a bowl with the garlic, chile powder, chile flakes, cumin, salt, and oil. Spread in a shallow roasting pan and roast until tender, 1 to 1 1/2 hours, stirring occasionally. Dress with chopped cilantro and lime juice. Serves 4.

Red Roasted Vegetable Skewers

The vegetables can soak up flavor in the marinade all afternoon and be cooked right on the grill with the steaks or fish. Try whatever vegetables you love best.

1 Tbs. Chimayó chile powder
1/2 tsp. dried thyme
1/2 tsp. fresh rosemary, minced
1 tsp. Mexican oregano
1/2 tsp. salt
1/4 tsp. freshly ground black pepper
1 cup virgin olive oil
2 tsp. red wine vinegar
2 tsp. balsamic vinegar
1 lb. eggplant, peeled and
    cut in 1-inch chunks

1 1/4 lbs. zucchini, cut in
    1-inch chunks
12 cherry tomatoes
12 small boiling onions, peeled
1 red bell pepper, cut in
    1-inch chunks
1 green bell pepper, cut in
    1-inch chunks
1 Tbs. fresh thyme leaves, minced
1 Tbs. fresh rosemary leaves,
    minced

In a large glass bowl, stir together the chile powder, dried thyme, 1/2 teaspoon of rosemary, the oregano, salt, and pepper. Whisk in 1/2 cup of the olive oil, then the vinegars. Continue whisking, adding remaining olive oil in a steady stream. Toss the prepared vegetables in the marinade, cover the bowl with plastic wrap, and let stand 1 hour or up to 3 hours at room temperature.

At least 30 minutes before grilling, soak 12 to 16 bamboo skewers in water to cover. When the grill is hot, thread the vegetables on soaked bamboo skewers and arrange on the grill. Depending on the heat of your fire and the position of the skewers on the grill, they will probably be done in 10 to 20 minutes. The hotter the grill, the more often you should turn the skewers, brushing them with additional marinade to keep them moist. Sprinkle with fresh thyme and rosemary before serving. Serves 6 to 8.

Sautéed Kale with Chile Balsamic Dressing

This tender-crisp sauté, with a touch of sesame oil and sweet balsamic vinegar, can also be made with fresh chard or spinach.

3 lbs. fresh kale, washed
    and stemmed
2 tsp. salt
1 Tbs. vegetable oil
3 cloves garlic, minced
1 tsp. chile Caribe
2 1/2 Tbs. balsamic vinegar

2 Tbs. soy sauce
2 Tbs. sesame oil
Salt and freshly ground pepper,
    to taste
1 Tbs. sesame seeds,
    lightly toasted

Wash the kale in several changes of water to remove all sand and grit; then trim out the tough stems. Stack up the kale leaves and slice crosswise into strips about 1 inch wide. Bring a large pot of water to boil and add 2 teaspoons of salt. Toss in the kale in handfuls and simmer until crispy-tender, about 2 to 3 minutes. Pour the kale into a colander and drain well.

In a large, nonstick skillet, heat the vegetable oil over medium heat and sauté the garlic for 1 minute. Add the chile Caribe and sauté another minute. Stir in the balsamic vinegar, soy sauce, and sesame oil, and add the kale to the skillet. Cut off the flame under the skillet and toss the kale in the hot dressing, add salt and pepper to taste, and sprinkle with toasted sesame seeds. Serves 4 to 6.

Roasted Scarlet Potatoes

1 1/2 lbs. baking potatoes, scrubbed
2 Tbs. canola oil
1/2 tsp. sweet paprika
1 tsp. Chimayó chile powder

1/8 tsp. ground cumin
1/4 tsp. dried Mexican oregano
Salt and freshly ground pepper,
    to taste

Preheat the oven to 375 degrees. Cut the potatoes in half crosswise, then cut each half into 4 wedges. In a heavy, cast-iron skillet, heat the oil to moderately hot and stir in the ground spices. After 30 seconds, add the potato wedges, sprinkle with oregano and salt and pepper to taste, and toss the potatoes in the oil and spices to coat. Transfer the skillet to the hot oven and roast the potatoes about 40 minutes, turning occasionally, until tender and browned. Serves 4.

Sugar Peas with Orange Chile Butter

Try this orange chile butter with tender spring asparagus, too.

1 tsp. ancho or pasilla chile puree
  (see page 16)
1/8 tsp. cumin seeds, toasted
  and ground
1 tsp. grated orange rind
4 Tbs. unsalted butter, softened

2 tsp. freshly squeezed orange juice
Salt and freshly ground pepper,
  to taste
1 tsp. salt
1 lb. fresh sugar peas,
  washed and trimmed

In a small bowl, beat the chile puree, cumin, orange rind and orange juice into the softened butter. Add salt and pepper to taste, and set aside. Fill a medium skillet with water to a depth of 1 inch, add 1 teaspoon of salt and bring the water to a boil. Add the sugar peas and simmer until just crisp tender, about 3 minutes. Pour the sugar peas into a colander and drain well, return them to the dry skillet, and set over a medium flame. Scrape the orange chile butter into the skillet, and toss lightly until the peas are coated and heated through. Serve immediately. Serves 3 to 4.

Vegetable Chilaquilas

2 Tbs. vegetable oil
1/2 medium onion, diced
3/4 cup fresh or frozen corn kernels
1 large zucchini, sliced in 1/4-inch
    thick slices
1 large red bell pepper, roasted,
    peeled, seeded, and diced
1 tsp. cumin seeds, toasted
    and ground
1 tsp. Chimayó chile powder

Salt and freshly ground pepper,
    to taste
1/4 cup ricotta cheese
1 1/2 cups Monterey Jack cheese,
    shredded
1 fresh red jalapeño chile,
    seeded and minced
6 blue corn tortillas
1 cup Salsa Fresca (page 25)
3 Tbs. chopped fresh cilantro

Preheat the oven to 500 degrees. In a large, heavy skillet heat the oil on a medium flame, and sauté the onion until wilted, about 3 minutes. Add the corn and zucchini, turn the flame to medium high and sauté, stirring frequently, until the vegetables are slightly browned. Stir the roasted pepper, cumin, and chile powder into the vegetables, add salt and pepper to taste, and set aside.

Mix the ricotta, shredded cheese and minced jalapeño chile together, combining thoroughly. Butter a loaf pan, and line it with a layer of blue corn tortillas, using scissors to trim the tortillas to fit. Spread 1/2 of the Salsa Fresca over the tortillas, cover with 1/2 the vegetables, 1/2 the cheese mixture, and 1/2 the chopped cilantro. Repeat the layers, ending with cheese, cover the loaf pan tightly with foil, and bake 12 minutes. Remove the foil cover and continue baking until the dish is hot through and the cheese is golden brown. Let stand about 5 minutes before serving. Serves 6 to 8.

Chile Corn Pudding

A rich, creamy corn pudding is the perfect accompaniment for baked ham or grilled beef or pork.

2 Tbs. unsalted butter
1/2 medium white onion,
    finely chopped
1 small red bell pepper, seeded
    and finely chopped
2 cups fresh or frozen corn kernels
2 tsp. Chimayó chile powder
1/2 tsp. cumin seeds, toasted
    and ground

1 tsp. sugar
1 tsp. salt
2 pinches freshly ground black
    pepper
2 cups whole milk, scalded
3 eggs, lightly beaten

Preheat the oven to 350 degrees, and butter a 2-quart casserole or baking dish. In a large heavy skillet, melt the butter and sauté the onion and red pepper until soft, about 5 minutes. Add the corn kernels and sauté over medium heat until the vegetables are beginning to brown lightly. Stir in the chile powder, cumin, sugar, salt, and pepper and continue to cook for 2 minutes. Set aside to cool slightly.

In a large mixing bowl, pour the hot scalded milk into the beaten eggs, stirring constantly until well combined. Stir the corn mixture into the eggs and milk, then pour the pudding into the prepared casserole. Set the casserole in a roasting pan, and pour boiling water into the pan to reach about 1 inch up the sides of the casserole. Put the roasting pan in the oven and bake the pudding about 45 minutes, until the custard is nearly set and the top is golden. Remove the casserole from the water bath and set aside about 10 minutes before serving. Serves 6 to 8.

Eggs and Cheese

Chama Camp Soufflé
with Chile-Cinnamon Honey Butter

If you're trekking in the wilds, you can prepare the soufflé batter at home and take it with you in a covered plastic container (it holds up well for at least 24 hours). If you're cooking over a campfire or an outdoor grill, put a lid on the iron skillet to hold in heat. This gourmet camp breakfast treat is best served on the banks of the Chama River, but it tastes almost as good on a Sunday morning at home!

6 slices good, thick bacon
6 eggs
2 cups sweet milk
1 cup flour

2 Tbs. sugar
3/4 tsp. salt
1/2 cup grated mild cheese
   (cheddar or Monterey Jack)

HONEY BUTTER

1/4 lb. butter, softened
1/4 cup honey
1 tsp. cinnamon

1 tsp. Chimayó chile powder,
   or to taste

Preheat the oven to 375 degrees (or stoke up the campfire). Cook the bacon until crisp and drain, reserving the drippings. Strain about 1/4 cup of bacon drippings into a cast-iron iron skillet 10 to 12 inches in diameter (if you used the skillet to cook the bacon, scrub it out so the soufflé won't stick). Put the skillet in the oven or on the grill to heat while you prepare the batter. Mix the eggs and milk in a blender on medium speed for a minute, or whisk together thoroughly in a bowl. Gradually add the flour, sugar, and salt, blending well after each addition. Pull the skillet out of the oven, sprinkle the crumbled bacon into the skillet and pour the batter over the bacon. Sprinkle the cheese evenly over the top of the soufflé and return the skillet to the oven, or covered, to the grill, for about 30 minutes, or until the soufflé is puffed and brown. Meanwhile, cream the honey, cinnamon, and chile powder into the softened butter and taste for just the "sweet" and "heat" that suits your fancy. When the soufflé emerges, cut it into wedges and serve it with a dollop of sweet, spicy butter on top. Serves 6.

Chimayó Chile Cheese Casserole

This casserole can be varied easily with additions such as cooked chicken or ground beef, or cooked, cubed potatoes for a vegetarian meal.

2 Tbs. butter, softened

8 to 12 white corn or flour tortillas
(depending on size)

1 lb. sage sausage or chorizo,
cooked and drained

1 medium onion, chopped and
lightly sautéed in butter

3 poblano chiles, roasted, peeled,
seeded, and chopped (optional)

3¹/2 cups mixed Monterey Jack and
cheddar cheeses, grated

1 cup Chimayó Red Sauce
(page 27)

6 eggs, beaten

1 tsp. salt

2 cups sweet milk

Preheat the oven to 350 degrees. Thoroughly butter a 132 92 2 glass baking dish and line it with the tortillas, overlapping them to cover the bottom and sides of the pan. Cover the tortillas with the well-drained sausage, sautéed onion, chopped chiles, and 2¹/2 cups of the grated cheese. Pour ¹/2 cup of Chimayó Red Sauce over the cheese. In a large bowl, whisk together the eggs, salt, and milk and pour the mixture over the cheese. Sprinkle the dish with the remaining cup of shredded cheese. Cover the dish with foil and bake about 30 minutes. Remove the foil and continue baking until the top is nicely colored and the custard has set, about 10 or 15 minutes. Remove the dish from the oven and let cool about 15 minutes; serve with the remaining Chimayó Red Sauce on the side. Serves 8 to 10.

Christmas Hash

Transform your leftover holiday bird into New Mexico-style "Christmas Hash"—with the flavor of both red and green chiles.

1 large onion, chopped
1/2 fresh red jalapeño, seeded
   and minced (or to taste)
3 Tbs. butter
2 cups cooked turkey, diced
1 cup sage sausage or chorizo,
   cooked and drained (optional)
3 green chiles, roasted, peeled,
   seeded, and chopped
   (about 1/2 cup)

2 Tbs. fresh cilantro leaves,
   chopped
1 scallion, chopped fine
Salt and cracked black pepper
1 cup of your favorite red sauce
6 to 8 tortillas
6 to 8 eggs

In a large skillet, sauté the onion and minced jalapeño lightly in butter until just soft. Add the cooked turkey and sausage, green chiles, cilantro, and scallions. Heat the "hash" through and add salt and pepper to taste. Meanwhile, warm up the red sauce in a small saucepan, heat the tortillas (wrapped in foil in a hot oven for about 10 minutes should do it), and soft-scramble or poach the eggs with a little salt. When the crowd has gathered at the table, put a hot tortilla on each plate, cover the tortilla with a mound of turkey hash, top the hash with a serving of egg, and pour a generous dollop of warm red sauce over the top. Serves 6 to 8.

Spinach and Trout Enchiladas Benedict

An elegant brunch or luncheon dish for holidays and special occasions. If blue corn tortillas are not available in your area, thin white corn tortillas are the best substitute. In a pinch, a 10-ounce package of frozen chopped spinach (defrosted and squeezed dry) may be substituted for the fresh spinach, and good quality roasted red peppers packed in oil may be used in place of fresh roasted peppers.

12 thin blue corn tortillas, warmed
2 Tbs. butter
1 lb. fresh spinach leaves, washed,
   trimmed, and sliced
1 tsp. freshly squeezed lemon juice
1/8 tsp. freshly grated nutmeg
Salt and cracked black pepper
1 lb. smoked trout fillets,
   skinned and flaked

3 roasted red bell peppers, peeled,
   seeded, and sliced into strips
1 1/2 cups Monterey Jack cheese,
   shredded
6 Tbs. heavy cream
6 eggs
2 cups Chipotle Hollandaise Sauce
   (page 23)

Preheat the oven to 300 degrees. Wrap the tortillas in foil and warm in the oven about 10 or 15 minutes. Butter a 132 92 2 glass baking dish and set aside. Melt 2 tablespoons of butter in a large skillet; toss in all the sliced spinach leaves at once, sprinkle with lemon juice, nutmeg, and salt and pepper, and cover. Cook the spinach until just wilted, and drain thoroughly. Remove one warm tortilla at a time to a large plate and spoon a portion of spinach, flaked trout, roasted pepper, and cheese (reserving 1/2 cup) down the center of the tortilla. Quickly roll the warm tortilla tightly around the filling and place in the glass baking dish, seam-side down. When all of the enchiladas have been rolled, sprinkle the cream and remaining 1/2 cup of cheese evenly over the tops of the enchiladas. Bake just until the enchiladas are warmed through and the cheese is melted and golden, about 15 or 20 minutes (do not overbake). Meanwhile, carefully poach six eggs. Put two enchiladas on each warmed plate, perch a poached egg on top, and dress with a little Chipotle Hollandaise Sauce. Serves 6.

Red Polenta with Chiles and Cheese

This hearty chile-cheese polenta can be made a day or two ahead of the final baking, and freezes beautifully baked or raw. You may prefer to substitute more chicken broth (or just water) for the wine; and pasilla chile puree (page 16) may be substituted for the ancho chile puree.

3 Tbs. butter, softened
1 1/2 cups rich chicken broth
1 1/2 cups dry white wine
1/2 tsp. salt
1 1/2 cups yellow cornmeal
2 Tbs. unsalted butter, softened
1 Tbs. ancho chile puree,
   or to taste (see page 16)

1/2 cup freshly grated Romano
   or Parmesan cheese
1 Tbs. fresh sage leaves,
   minced (or 2 tsp. dried)
2 Tbs. fresh parsley, chopped
1 cup Monterey Jack cheese, grated
1 Tbs. butter, softened
3 Tbs. cream

Preheat the oven to 400 degrees. Generously butter a 2 1/2 quart gratin dish or other shallow baking pan, and refrigerate. Bring the broth and wine with salt to a rolling boil in a big, heavy saucepan. Add the cornmeal to the boiling liquid in a slow stream, whisking constantly; reduce the heat to medium-low and simmer about 5 minutes until the mixture begins to thicken and pull away from sides of pan. Take the pan off the heat and immediately stir in the unsalted butter, chile puree, half of the Romano or Parmesan cheese, the sage, and the parsley. Remove the gratin dish from the refrigerator. Working quickly, stir the grated Monterey Jack cheese into the polenta with a heavy wooden spoon and push the mixture into the buttered gratin dish, spreading it evenly into the pan and smoothing the top with the wooden spoon. Dot the polenta with butter, and sprinkle the cream and the remaining Romano or Parmesan cheese over the top. Bake about 25 or 30 minutes, until golden brown on top. Serves 8 to 10.

Chipotle Shirred Eggs and Artichokes

A decorative brunch buffet dish, these baked eggs can be made in a large casserole or individual ramekins.

1 Tbs. chipotle en adobo, pureed
1/2 cup sour cream
1 large head Romaine lettuce,
   washed and dried
1 Tbs. butter
1/8 tsp. cumin seeds, toasted
   and ground
Salt and freshly ground pepper,
   to taste

1 Tbs. butter
8 large cooked artichoke hearts,
   trimmed and chokes removed
8 large eggs
1/4 cup cream
1 cup mild cheddar cheese, shredded

Preheat the oven to 325 degrees. Whisk the pureed chipotle en adobo into the sour cream in a small bowl and set aside at room temperature. Wash and dry the Romaine leaves, stack them up and slice them crosswise very thin. Heat 1 tablespoon of butter in a large skillet, and gently sauté the Romaine with the ground cumin and salt and pepper to taste just until wilted; drain thoroughly and set aside. Melt the other tablespoon of butter in the skillet and gently sauté the artichoke hearts until they are hot through; set aside and keep warm. Heavily butter a deep-sided glass or ceramic casserole dish at least 10 inches square (or 8 individual ramekins) and place inside a larger pan, such as a roasting pan. Spread the Romaine evenly over the bottom of the casserole dish, or divide equally among the ramekins. Arrange the artichoke hearts evenly over the Romaine, nestling them into the Romaine so they are stable. Carefully crack the eggs, one at a time, into a small bowl or cup and slip each egg onto an artichoke heart with the yolk resting in the cup of the heart. Pour the cream around the eggs. Pour enough boiling water into the roasting pan to reach well up the sides of the casserole or ramekins, and put into the oven for 15 minutes. Slide the pan out of the oven and sprinkle the eggs with shredded cheese, then drizzle with the chipotle sour cream. Return the pan to the oven until the eggs are set and the cheese has melted, about 10 minutes. Serves 8.

Huevos Rancheros San Miguel

There are many variations of this simple dish, the only essentials being tortillas, fried or poached eggs, and a great chile sauce. This recipe gets its rich flavor from red chile sauce of San Miguel de Allende in central Mexico. Dress it up for brunch with garnishes such as sliced avocados, crumbled chorizo, fresh chopped lettuce, and tomato.

12 small corn tortillas (freshly
    made, if possible)
3 slices bacon
1 small white onion, diced
3 medium potatoes, peeled, cooked,
    and diced
1½ cups San Miguel Red Sauce
    (page 28)

2 Tbs. butter
6 large eggs
1 cup crumbled fresh white cheese,
    or shredded Monterey Jack
    cheese
3 radishes, scrubbed and
    sliced thin
6 pitted black olives, sliced thin

Wrap the tortillas in foil and warm in a hot oven. Cook the bacon slowly in a heavy skillet until crisp; remove, drain, and crumble the bacon, and set aside. In the fat remaining in the skillet, sauté the diced onion over medium heat about 5 minutes. Add the diced potatoes to the pan and sauté until the potatoes are browned. Remove the potatoes and onions to a bowl and keep warm. Pour the San Miguel Red Sauce into the skillet and heat. In a separate skillet, lightly fry the eggs in butter. To assemble, place two hot tortillas overlapping on each of 6 plates, spoon fried potatoes and onions onto the tortillas, top the potatoes with fried eggs, spoon San Miguel Red Sauce over the eggs, sprinkle cheese over the Red Sauce and crumbled bacon over the cheese. Garnish each plate with radishes and olives and serve immediately. Serves 6.

Hot Cheese and Portabello Sandwich with Chipotle Mayonnaise

Already a meal in itself, it can be made even more substantial by adding sautéed crab meat and sliced avocado to the filling.

$^{1}/_{4}$ cup balsamic vinegar
$^{1}/_{4}$ cup virgin olive oil
2 tsp. finely minced garlic
A pinch of salt, or to taste
2 large Portabello mushrooms, cleaned and sliced
1 10-inch round loaf focaccia or other herbed flat bread

1 large red bell pepper, roasted, peeled, and sliced
1 Tbs. fresh parsley, chopped
4 slices good Swiss cheese
$^{1}/_{4}$ cup Roasted Garlic Chile Mayonnaise (page 23, substitute 1 tsp. pureed chipotle en adobo for Chimayó chile)

Mix the vinegar, olive oil, garlic, and salt in a medium bowl. Add the sliced mushrooms and marinate for 1 hour. Grill or sauté the mushrooms until cooked through but still firm. Slice the focaccia horizontally with a long bread knife. Arrange the mushrooms, roasted pepper slices, chopped parsley, and sliced cheese on the bottom half of the focaccia, and put it under a broiler until the cheese is melted and bubbly. Spread the Chipotle Garlic Mayonnaise on the top half of the focaccia, and place on top of the broiled filling. Quarter the loaf with a sharp knife and serve the sandwich hot. Serves 4.

Red Chile Omelette

1 Tbs. butter
6 scallions, sliced
2 red bell peppers, roasted,
    peeled, seeded, and diced
1 tsp. Mexican oregano
1 Tbs. ancho or pasilla chile puree
    (see page 16)
1 tsp. chipotle en adobo,
    or to taste

8 to 10 eggs, lightly beaten
Salt and freshly ground pepper,
    to taste
2 Tbs. butter
1 cup shredded Monterey
    Jack cheese

Melt 1 tablespoon of butter in a 10-inch nonstick omelette pan and sauté the scallions until they are wilted. Add the diced red pepper, oregano, chile puree, and chipotle en adobo to the skillet and sauté another minute or two, then scrape into a bowl and set aside. Season the beaten eggs with salt and pepper to taste. Heat 2 tablespoons of butter in the omelette pan until hot and foaming, then pour in the eggs. Cook the omelette over medium heat until nearly set, lifting the sides carefully with a spatula every few minutes and tilting the pan to let eggs flow to the bottom of the pan. When the omelette is nearly done, spoon the sauteed vegetables and chiles evenly over 1/2 of the omelette, sprinkle the shredded cheese over the vegetables, and fold the other half of the omelette over the filling. Remove the pan from the heat and let sit for a few minutes to set the eggs and melt the cheese. Cut into wedges and serve, with lots of hot buttered toast on the side. Serves 6.

Spicy Southwestern Quiche

For elegant party fare, add fresh-cooked shrimp or sautéed scallops.

Pastry for a 10-inch pie pan
2 Tbs. butter
1 bunch fresh spinach,
   washed and trimmed
Salt and cracked black pepper
1/8 tsp. freshly grated nutmeg
4 scallions, minced
1 fresh red jalapeño or Fresno chile,
   seeded and minced
   (to taste)
1/8 tsp. cumin seeds, toasted
   and ground

1/2 tsp. Mexican oregano
2 medium tomatoes, peeled, seeded,
   and diced
3 eggs, lightly beaten
1 1/2 cups light cream or half
   and half
Salt and cracked black pepper
1/2 cup Monterey Jack cheese,
   shredded

Preheat the oven to 375 degrees. Line the pie pan with pastry, line the pastry with foil and fill with enough raw rice to weigh it down. Put the pastry in the oven for 10 minutes, then remove from the oven, remove the foil and rice, and let the partially cooked pastry shell cool in the pie pan on a rack.

Melt 1 tablespoon of butter in a deep skillet over medium high heat. Pile all the washed and trimmed spinach into the skillet, sprinkle with salt, pepper, and nutmeg, cover and cook until fully wilted (lift the cover and stir every minute or two to cook evenly), about 5 minutes. Let the spinach cool, then drain very thoroughly (squeezing out all moisture) and chop. Set the spinach aside. Melt the remaining tablespoon of butter in the skillet and sauté the scallions and minced chiles until wilted, about 5 minutes. Toss in the cumin, oregano, and diced tomatoes and sauté until the mixture is cooked through and the moisture from the tomatoes has evaporated, about 5 or 10 minutes. In a large bowl, mix the eggs with the cream, stir in the chopped spinach, the tomato mixture and half the shredded cheese and mix thoroughly. Taste for seasoning and add salt and pepper to taste. Pour the mixture into the prepared pie shell and sprinkle the top with the remaining shredded cheese. Bake the quiche in a 375-degree oven until the filling is set and the top is golden brown, about 30 minutes. Cool slightly before cutting. Serves 6.

Fish and Shellfish

Ancho Chile Crab Cakes

These crab cakes may be served as is, or with a roasted garlic mayonnaise or a remoulade sauce on the side. This recipe will also make about 3 dozen tiny crab cake appetizers.

4 cups crab meat (about 1 1/2 lbs.),
  picked over
1 cup fresh bread crumbs
2 large eggs
2/3 cup heavy cream
2 Tbs. ancho chile puree
  (see page 16)

3 tsp. Worcestershire sauce
3 tsp. fresh parsley, finely minced
1 Tbs. shallots, finely minced
3 Tbs. unsalted butter

In a large bowl, combine the crab meat and the bread crumbs. In another bowl whisk together the eggs, cream, and chile puree. Add the cream mixture and the remaining ingredients (except butter) to the crab mixture and combine well. Melt the butter in a heavy, nonstick sauté pan over moderate heat. Gently pat the crab mixture into 8 flattened cakes. When the butter has foamed, sauté the crab cakes 3 or 4 minutes on each side until golden brown and cooked through. Serve with lemon wedges, and a sauce if you like. Serves 4.

Chile-Rubbed Catfish
with Southwest Remoulade

This peppery chile rub is also good on fresh tuna or any other firm-fleshed fish. You can broil the chile-rubbed filets inside on a rack 5 to 6 inches from the heat source (watch carefully to avoid burning the chile crust). The remoulade sauce can be made ahead, and keeps several days in the refrigerator.

2 cups mayonnaise,
  preferably homemade
1 Tbs. Dijon mustard
1 tsp. freshly squeezed lime juice
1 clove garlic, finely minced
1/2 tsp. Chimayó chile powder
2 Tbs. minced gherkins or
  sour pickles
2 Tbs. capers, drained and chopped
1/4 cup fresh parsley, finely minced
2 Tbs. chives or chervil,
  finely minced
4 or 5 anchovy filets, minced

Salt and freshly ground pepper,
  to taste
1 Tbs. Chimayó chile powder
1/2 Tbs. chipotle chile, stemmed,
  seeded, and crushed
2 tsp. freshly ground black pepper
2 Tbs. minced fresh thyme leaves
1 Tbs. minced fresh garlic
1 tsp. salt
1 1/2 lbs. catfish filets, 1/2-inch thick
2 Tbs. peanut oil
1 large lime, cut in 6 wedges

Thoroughly combine the first 11 ingredients (for the remoulade) in a medium glass bowl; cover and refrigerate at least 2 hours before serving. In a small bowl combine the chile powder, crushed chipotle chile, black pepper, thyme, garlic, and salt. Rinse the catfish filets and pat dry. Rub the chile mixture thoroughly into both sides of the filets, put them in a glass dish, cover with plastic wrap, and let marinate about 30 minutes at room temperature or refrigerate up to 3 hours. Bring the fish back to room temperature before cooking.

Prepare your grill for a hot fire. When the coals are covered with gray ash, brush a fish-grilling rack with the peanut oil and lay the filets on the rack. Grill the fish over hot coals, turning once, until done through, about 5 to 7 minutes. Serve the catfish with lime wedges and chile remoulade sauce on the side. Serves 6.

Chile-Crusted Tuna Wasabi

Note that searing the spice-crusted steaks over high heat releases very strong fumes, which can lead to stinging eyes and burning throats. We recommend cooking on an outdoor grill, unless you have a very good vent over your kitchen range.

$^1/_2$ tsp. wasabi powder
$^1/_2$ cup plain yogurt
1 oz. good tequila
1 tsp. freshly squeezed lime juice
1 Tbs. cilantro leaves, minced
2 dried chipotle chiles, stemmed,
    seeded, and crushed
$^1/_4$ tsp. coarse salt

$^1/_2$ tsp. crushed black peppercorns
$^1/_2$ tsp. dried thyme
1 tsp. cumin seeds, toasted and
    ground
2 lbs. fresh tuna steak,
    cut 1 inch thick
2 Tbs. fresh lime zest

Put the wasabi powder in a small bowl and work it into a paste with 1 or 2 teaspoons of water. Mix in the yogurt, tequila, lime juice, and cilantro. Cover the bowl with plastic wrap and set aside or refrigerate until ready to serve.

In a small bowl, crush together the chiles, salt, pepper, thyme, and cumin. Coat the tuna steaks all over with the spice mixture. If you are cooking outside, prepare the grill for a very hot fire. When the grill is ready, heat a large cast iron skillet to smoking hot on a kitchen burner, then take it outside and set it on the grill rack. In the hot skillet, sear the tuna steaks to medium rare, 4 to 5 minutes per side. Sprinkle the steaks with fresh lime zest and serve them with wasabi sauce on the side. Serves 4.

Chile-Buttered Shrimp

4 cloves garlic, finely minced
1 Tbs. cilantro leaves, chopped
2 tsp. Mexican oregano
2 tsp. Chimayó chile powder
$^1/_4$ tsp. freshly ground black pepper
$1^1/_2$ tsp. salt
1 tsp. Tabasco or other hot sauce

1 Tbs. Worcestershire sauce
2 Tbs. freshly squeezed lime juice
$^3/_4$ lb. unsalted butter, softened
2 lbs. large shrimp, peeled
    and deveined
1 bunch scallions, thinly sliced

Preheat the oven to 500 degrees. Combine garlic, cilantro, oregano, chile powder, pepper, salt, hot sauce, Worcestershire sauce, and lime juice in the bowl of a food processor and pulse to a puree. Add the softened butter and process to a smooth blend. Spread the cleaned shrimp in a baking dish just large enough to hold them in one layer and sprinkle the scallions over the shrimp. Drop the blended butter by teaspoons evenly over the shrimp. Put the shrimp in the oven and bake for about 5 minutes until done. Spoon the shrimp and plenty of butter sauce onto four warmed plates, and serve immediately with crusty, hot bread. Serves 4.

ʃ ʃ ʃ

Pasilla Striped Bass Baked with Spinach

This easy recipe works well with other firm, white-fleshed fish and with a favorite red chile sauce served on the side.

2 lbs. fresh striped bass filet,
   cut into serving pieces
2 garlic cloves, minced
1/4 cup fresh parsley, chopped
1 Tbs. pasilla chile puree
   (see page 16)

1/4 cup virgin olive oil
1 bunch spinach, thoroughly
   washed, trimmed, and dried
1/4 tsp. freshly ground nutmeg
Salt and freshly ground pepper,
   to taste

Preheat the oven to 450 degrees. Rinse and dry the fish. Mix the garlic, parsley, chile puree, and 1 tablespoon of olive oil in a small bowl. Smear the puree evenly over the fish pieces. Brush 2 tablespoons of olive oil in the bottom of a glass roasting pan just large enough to hold the fish comfortably in one layer. Stack the cleaned, trimmed fresh spinach leaves and with a sharp knife slice the leaves crosswise into chiffonade about 1/8 of an inch wide. Spread the chiffonade in the bottom of the roasting pan, and sprinkle with the grated nutmeg and salt and pepper to taste. Arrange the bass filets in the pan on the bed of chiffonade and drizzle with remaining olive oil. Roast the fish until tender, about 20 to 30 minutes. Remove the bass pieces to a platter, cover and keep warm. Drain the spinach and press out excess moisture. Divide the spinach among 4 to 6 warm plates, top with a piece of bass, and drizzle with red chile sauce, if desired. Serves 4 to 6.

Fiery Red Snapper with Fennel

Everything but the final assembly can be done a day ahead. Any mild, white-fleshed fish can be substituted for the red snapper.

2 fennel bulbs, trimmed and
   sliced thin
1 Tbs. light olive oil
1 large red onion, finely chopped
2 medium red bell peppers, seeded
   and finely chopped
2 medium celery stalks, finely
   chopped
2 medium scallions, minced
3 cloves garlic, minced
2 Tbs. fresh ginger, minced

2 tsp. red serrano chiles,
   seeded and minced
4 large tomatoes, peeled
   and crushed
2 tsp. thyme leaves, minced
1/4 tsp. ground cloves
Salt and freshly ground pepper,
   to taste
4 red snapper filets, 6 or 7 oz.
   each, 3/4 inch thick

Preheat the oven to 450 degrees. Trim and slice the fennel, steam in a colander over boiling water until crisp-tender, about 4 minutes, and set aside. Heat the oil in a large skillet and sauté the onion, bell pepper, celery, scallions, garlic, ginger, and serrano chile over medium high heat for 7 minutes. Stir in the crushed tomatoes, thyme and cloves and bring the sauce to a boil. Reduce the heat to low and simmer the sauce until it has thickened slightly, about 5 minutes. Taste the sauce for seasoning and add salt and pepper. Stir the reserved fennel slices into the sauce, and pour the sauce into a deep-sided baking dish just large enough to hold the fish filets without crowding. Arrange the snapper filets over the sauce, cover the pan tightly with foil and bake the fish for 10 to 15 minutes until it is just cooked through and the sauce is bubbling. Serves 4.

New Mexico Chile-Smoked Salmon

The spicy rub can be used with any large, firm-fleshed fish that you like to grill or smoke. The fish is delicious as is, or served with a fresh tropical fruit salsa.

4 Tbs. grated onion
2 tsp. ground cloves
2 tsp. freshly ground black pepper
2 tsp. cayenne
2 tsp. brown sugar
4 tsp. fresh thyme leaves, minced

2 tsp. ground canela
1/2 tsp. nutmeg, freshly ground
2 tsp. Chimayó chile powder
3 lbs. salmon filets,
      skinned and trimmed

Mix rub ingredients thoroughly in small bowl. Wipe the salmon filets dry, and rub all over with spice mix. Set the salmon aside in a glass baking pan, covered, in the refrigerator for 1 hour or up to 4 hours; bring to room temperature before grilling. Prepare a covered grill or smoker, bringing the temperature to a stable 200 degrees. Place the salmon on a fish-grilling rack, place the rack in the grill or smoker and cover. Cook the fish about 20 minutes, then turn. Cook the fish another 20 to 30 minutes, or until it is cooked through and the meat flakes easily. Serves 4 to 6.

Pan-Fried San Juan Trout

Sportsmen from around the world travel to northern New Mexico's San Juan River to fly-fish for trophy trout. This recipe will transform any fresh trout into award-winning dinner fare.

$^1/_2$ cup all-purpose flour, sifted
1 tsp. Chimayó chile powder,
   or to taste
1 tsp. salt
1 pinch freshly ground
   black pepper
8 small trout filets, 3 to 4 oz. each,
   rinsed and dried

2 Tbs. vegetable oil
3 to 4 Tbs. unsalted butter,
   softened
$^1/_4$ cup fresh parsley, chopped
1 Tbs. cilantro leaves, chopped
Juice of 2 lemons

Mix the sifted flour with the chile powder, salt, and pepper and spread out on a flat plate. Dredge the trout filets in the flour, and lay out on a flat dish or baking rack. Heat the vegetable oil to hot, but not smoking, in a heavy nonstick skillet. Pan fry the filets in the hot oil for about 1 minute on each side, then add the softened butter and cook until the filets are golden, another minute on each side. With a slotted spatula, remove the filets to 4 warmed plates. Toss the parsley, cilantro, and lemon juice into the skillet and whisk together 1 or 2 minutes until hot. Pour the sauce over the trout filets, garnish with parsley and lemon wedges and serve. Serves 4.

Cold Poached Salmon
with Orange Chipotle Cream

This dish can be prepared a day ahead. The fish can be poached whole, rather than filleted, and served on a buffet platter.

1/2 cup celery, chopped
1/2 cup carrot, chopped
1/2 cup onion, chopped
1 lemon, sliced
3 sprigs fresh parsley
1/2 tsp. salt
2 lbs. fresh salmon filets, trimmed
1 cup dry white wine
1/3 cup shallots, minced
3/4 cup freshly squeezed orange
   juice, strained

3/4 cup dry white wine
3/4 cup heavy cream
1 tsp. sauce from chipotles en
   adobo, or to taste
Salt, to taste
1/2 bunch fresh spinach, thoroughly
   washed, trimmed, and dried
1 bunch chives, washed, dried, and
   cut into 3-inch lengths

Butter a small, covered roasting pan and strew the chopped vegetables, lemon, parsley, and salt on the bottom. Cut the salmon filet in half and wrap each half in cheesecloth, leaving long ends for lifting the fish out of the poaching liquid. Arrange the wrapped filets on top of the vegetables, skin side up, with the long ends of the cheesecloth draped over the edge of the roaster. Pour 1 cup wine over the fish, then add just enough water to the pan so that the fish is covered by the liquid. Set the roaster over a medium flame and bring to a simmer, then cover and turn heat low. Poach the fish at a very low simmer for 7 minutes. Carefully lift the filets and turn them over, and continue to poach another 5 to 7 minutes. When the fish is just cooked through, lift the filets out of the broth and set aside to cool at room temperature. When the fish is cool and firm enough to handle, remove the skin and cut the filets into 6 neat serving portions. Place the fish in a glass dish, cover tightly with plastic wrap, and chill several hours.

Bring shallots, orange juice, and 3/4 cup wine to a boil in a heavy, enameled saucepan and reduce to 1/2 cup. Add the cream and the adobo sauce and continue to cook over medium heat, stirring from time to time, until reduced to 1 cup, about 45 minutes. Cool the sauce to room temperature. Taste and adjust seasonings. Stack the cleaned, trimmed fresh spinach leaves and with a sharp knife slice the leaves crosswise into chiffonade about 1/16 of an inch wide. Make a bed of chiffonade across the center of each of 6 service plates. Place a serving of cold poached salmon on top of the chiffonade on each plate. Nap each serving of salmon with chipotle orange cream, and strew fresh chives on top of the sauce. Serves 6.

Scallops with Chile Pistachio Pesto

Pistachio nuts are a natural variation from piñon nuts for a chile-spiked pesto. Serve them with your favorite fresh pasta.

1/2 cup cilantro leaves, chopped
1 1/2 cups fresh parsley, chopped
1 clove garlic, minced
1 tsp. grated lemon zest
1/4 cup freshly squeezed lemon juice
1/2 tsp. cumin seed, toasted
2 tsp. Chimayó chile powder
1/4 tsp. freshly ground black pepper
1/4 tsp. salt
2 Tbs. extra virgin olive oil,
* or more to taste*

1/3 cup shelled, chopped pistachio
* nuts (roasted or raw)*
1/2 cup all-purpose flour
1/4 tsp. salt
1 1/2 lbs. sea scallops,
* rinsed and dried*
1 Tbs. unsalted butter
2 Tbs. olive oil

Combine the first 11 ingredients (for the pesto) in the bowl of a food processor and pulse until the mixture is thick and well combined. Shake the flour and salt together in a heavy-duty plastic bag, toss in the scallops a few at a time, and shake to coat all over. Heat the butter and oil to hot (but not smoking) in a nonstick skillet. Sauté the scallops, in batches, about 3 minutes on each side until golden brown and cooked through. Combine the scallops with the pesto and serve immediately. Serves 4.

Savory Boiled Shrimp with Jalapeño Salsa

Serve with a casual supper. Be sure to provide bowls for the shrimp shells, lots of napkins, and plenty of hot tortillas and cold beer.

1 cup bottled cocktail sauce,
  or your own
2 Tbs. freshly squeezed lime juice
1/2 tsp. soy sauce
1/4 cup prepared horseradish,
  or to taste
2 fresh Fresno or red jalapeño
  chiles, seeded and minced
1 fresh red serrano chile, seeded and
  minced
3 cloves garlic, peeled and minced
1 small red onion, minced
1/4 cup cilantro leaves, chopped
Dash of Tabasco or other hot sauce,
  to taste
Salt and freshly ground pepper,
  to taste
1 Tbs. fennel seed

1 Tbs. cumin seed
1 Tbs. coriander seed
1 Tbs. mustard seed
1 Tbs. black peppercorns
1 Tbs. whole cloves
2 Tbs. olive oil
1 medium red onion, chopped
1 whole head of garlic, halved
  crosswise
3 fresh red jalapeño chiles,
  seeded and chopped
Zest of one large orange
3 bottles of Negro Modelo
  or other dark beer
2 bay leaves
32 large fresh shrimp in shell
  (about 2 lbs.), rinsed

Prepare the salsa in a small bowl. Whisk together the cocktail sauce, lime juice, soy sauce, and horseradish; stir in the chiles, garlic, onion, and cilantro. Taste for seasoning and adjust the kick with hot sauce. Add salt and pepper to taste. Cover the sauce and chill until ready to serve.

Heat a large kettle over medium heat. Add the fennel, cumin, coriander, mustard seed, peppercorns, and cloves to the kettle and toast for about 30 seconds, stirring. Add the olive oil, onion, garlic, chiles, and orange zest and sauté the mixture until the onions have softened and begin to brown slightly. Stir in the beer and bay leaves and bring to a boil. Add the shrimp and return the pot to a boil. Quickly test a shrimp for doneness. If done, drain the shrimps and divide them among 4 plates. Serve at once with jalapeño salsa for dipping. Serves 4.

Three-Chile Roasted Grouper

This easy dish goes well with fresh corn on the cob and a summer salad on the side. If you can't readily obtain all three types of chiles, 1 or 2 of them will do.

2 lbs. fresh grouper or monkfish
    filets, cut into serving pieces
Salt and freshly ground pepper,
    to taste
2 garlic cloves, minced
1/4 cup fresh parsley, chopped
1 tsp. cumin seeds, toasted
    and ground
1/2 tsp. coriander seeds, toasted and
    ground
1 pinch of ground cloves

1/4 tsp. ground cinnamon
1/4 tsp. cayenne powder
1/2 Tbs. ancho chile puree
    (see page 16)
1/2 Tbs. pasilla chile puree
    (see page 16)
1/2 Tbs. mulatto chile puree
    (see page 16)
1/4 cup virgin olive oil
2 large ripe tomatoes, peeled,
    seeded and diced

Preheat the oven to 450 degrees. Rinse and dry the fish and sprinkle lightly with salt and pepper. Mix the garlic, parsley, ground spices, and chile purees in a bowl. Spread the puree evenly over the fish pieces. Brush half the olive oil in the bottom of a glass roasting pan just large enough to hold the fish comfortably in one layer. Spread half the diced tomato in the bottom of the roasting pan, arrange the filets in the pan on the bed of diced tomatoes, top with remaining tomatoes, and drizzle with remaining olive oil. Roast the fish until tender, about 20 to 30 minutes. Serves 4.

Poultry

Clay-Baked Red Duck

This recipe calls for a whole farm-raised duck. If you use wild ducks, you will need 2 or 3 of them as they generally weigh under 2 pounds (get somebody else to pluck them!). Slow-baking the bird in clay renders out the fat without spattering the oven; yields succulent, tender meat; and is simple and easy for the cook.

2 or 3 large cloves of garlic, crushed
   with a tsp. of salt
2 Tbs. virgin olive oil
2 Tbs. Marsala or brandy (optional)
1 Tbs. Chimayó red chile powder
1 Tbs. chipotle chile powder

1 whole duck (thawed,
   if purchased frozen)
2 large onions
1/2 cup Chile-Cherry Glaze
   (page 20)

Mix the crushed garlic, olive oil, Marsala or brandy, and chile powders in a small bowl and set aside. Wash the duck, dry it thoroughly with paper towels, and cut it into serving pieces with poultry shears or a sharp, heavy knife. If using wild duck, pour 1/2 cup of red wine or vinegar over pieces, let stand 5 minutes; then rinse and dry. The procedure will remove some of the "gamey" taste. Use your fingers to gently loosen the skin from the meat on each duck piece to make a "pocket" and spread some of the chile marinade onto the meat under the skin, distributing the marinade evenly among the pieces. Set the duck aside in a glass dish to marinate for 30 minutes.

Fill both halves of a clay baker with water to soak for 30 minutes (the baker should be about the size of the duck). Slice the onions into thin rings and set aside. Preheat the oven to 325 degrees. Empty the water from the baker and spread about 2/3 of the onion rings over the bottom. Arrange the duck pieces on top of the onion rings, skin side up, and put the remaining onion rings on top of the duck. Cover the baker, and put it in the oven for 1 1/2 hours. Test the meat for doneness, it should still be rosy but the juices should run yellow; if you prefer your duck medium, let it bake another 1/2 hour. Remove the baker from the oven and let the duck rest in the baker for 10 or 15 minutes while you warm the Chile-Cherry Glaze. Remove the duck pieces to a warm platter, discarding the skin, and drizzle with warm Chile-Cherry Glaze. Serves 2 or 3.

Poblanos Rellenos with Turkey Picadillo

Chiles rellenos are often stuffed only with cheese, but this spicy picadillo offers a great way to use up the remains of the holiday bird.

3 Tbs. corn or vegetable oil
1 small onion, chopped fine
1 large carrot, finely diced
1 small zucchini, finely diced
2 or 3 garlic cloves, minced
1 Tbs. pasilla chile puree
    (see page 16)
2 cups peeled, seeded, chopped
    tomatoes
1/4 cup almonds, chopped and
    toasted

1/4 cup raisins
2 cups cooked turkey, diced
2 egg whites
1 whole egg
1 cup all-purpose flour
1/2 cup beer
4 large, fresh poblano chiles,
    roasted, peeled, seeded, and slit
1/2 lb. Monterey Jack cheese,
    shredded
3 or 4 Tbs. clarified butter

Heat the oil in a large, heavy skillet and sauté the onion, carrot, and zucchini until the onions are translucent. Add the garlic and continue cooking for 2 or 3 minutes. Add the pasilla chile puree, tomatoes, almonds, raisins, and turkey and cook slowly until the picadillo is very thick, about 20 or 30 minutes. Turn the picadillo into a glass bowl to cool, but do not chill. Wipe out the skillet.

Beat the egg whites to stiff peaks and set aside. Beat the whole egg, then gradually whip in the flour and the beer, alternating wet and dry ingredients, to make a thick batter. Gently fold in the whipped egg whites and chill the batter for 1 hour. Carefully stuff the roasted poblano chiles, distributing approximately 1/4 of the cheese and the picadillo into each chile (do not overstuff), and gently pulling the edges of the chile together over the filling. Put the stuffed chiles on a plate, seam-side down, and chill in the refrigerator for 15 or 20 minutes to firm the filling.

Preheat the oven to 350 degrees. Heat the clarified butter in a medium skillet until hot. Working carefully, dip the stuffed chiles one by one into the chilled batter to coat thoroughly, and put them in the pan of hot butter, seam-side down. Brown them for a few minutes on each side, turning them carefully, and transfer them to a baking sheet, seam-side up. Put them in the hot oven to heat through and melt the cheese, about 10 minutes. Serve the stuffed chiles with a little red chile sauce or tomato sauce and sour cream on the side. Serves 4.

Quick Turkey Mole

In central Mexico and the Yucatan, the Christmas feast is not complete without turkey mole poblano. The typical mole poblano includes a variety of chiles and the distinctive touch of chocolate, and takes approximately forever to prepare. The savor of this quick version will depend on the quality of the prepared mole sauce you buy. Serve turkey mole poblano with hot tortillas, black beans and a fresh salad of cool greens.

1 young turkey, about 8 to 10 lbs.	1/2 Tbs. salt
4 Tbs. lard or oil	4 peppercorns
1/2 cup each chopped onion,	4 to 6 Tbs. lard or oil
carrot, and celery	2 cups bottled mole poblano sauce
1 clove garlic, peeled	2 to 3 cups turkey broth
3 sprigs of parsley	4 Tbs. sesame seeds, toasted
1 bay leaf	

Cut the turkey into serving pieces, plus neck and back, with poultry shears or a good cleaver, reserving the giblets. In a large, heavy pot, brown the turkey pieces (except the giblets) in hot lard or oil. Add the reserved giblets, and the onion, carrot, celery, garlic, parsley, bay leaf, salt, and peppercorns to the pot. Cover the turkey and vegetables with water and bring to a boil over medium heat. Reduce the heat, cover the pot, and simmer for about an hour. Remove the turkey pieces (except neck, back, and giblets) to a glass dish, cover tightly, and set aside. Continue to simmer the turkey neck, back and giblets with the vegetables for about another hour. Strain and cool the turkey broth, and remove the fat.

In a large, heavy pot, heat the 4 to 6 tablespoons of lard or oil over medium high heat. Carefully scrape the prepared mole into the hot lard (it will spatter, so be careful!) and sauté for about 5 minutes, stirring constantly so the sauce will not scorch. Whisk 2 cups of turkey broth into the mole and combine thoroughly. Simmer for 20 or 30 minutes, adding more broth if the sauce seems too thick. Add the cooked turkey pieces to the sauce and simmer another 10 to 20 minutes to heat through. Sprinkle each serving with toasted sesame seeds. Serves 10.

Savory Stuffed Chicken Breasts

These breasts of chicken can be made ahead in batches and stored in the freezer, wrapped individually in plastic wrap and then aluminum foil. In a pinch, a 10-ounce package of frozen chopped spinach (defrosted and squeezed dry) may be substituted for the fresh spinach.

1 Tbs. unsalted butter
1 lb. fresh spinach leaves, washed, trimmed and sliced
1 tsp. freshly squeezed lemon juice
1/8 tsp. freshly grated nutmeg
Salt and cracked black pepper
1 cup chorizo, cooked and drained
1 medium onion, finely chopped
1/2 lb. whole milk ricotta cheese
1/4 lb. Asiago or Monterey Jack cheese, grated
1/4 lb. mild goat cheese
2 Tbs. chipotles en adobo sauce, pureed

1 egg, slightly beaten
1/2 cup toasted piñon nuts or diced water chestnuts
1/4 cup fresh parsley, coarsely chopped
1 Tbs. mixed fresh herbs (for example, oregano, summer savory, and chervil)
Salt and freshly ground pepper, to taste
8 chicken breast halves (boned, with skin on)
1/2 cup butter, melted

Preheat the oven to 350 degrees. Melt 2 tablespoons of butter in a large skillet; toss in all the sliced spinach leaves at once, sprinkle with lemon juice, nutmeg and salt and pepper, and cover. Cook the spinach until just wilted, and drain thoroughly, squeezing out excess moisture with your hands. Cook the chorizo in a heavy skillet until browned and drain, reserving the fat. Return 2 tablespoons of the chorizo fat to the skillet, and sauté the chopped onions in the fat until soft. Combine the cooked spinach, chorizo and onion with remaining ingredients (except the chicken and melted butter) in a large bowl and mix well. Add salt and pepper and taste for seasoning (the mixture should taste highly seasoned before cooking, as the cheeses are quite mild).

Place each chicken breast half skin side up on a cutting board. Trim away excess fat, carefully loosen the skin from one edge of the breast, and stuff 1/2 cup to 2/3 cup of the filling under the skin. Wrap the skin tightly over the filling and tuck under the breast, forming an even, rounded, dome shape. Brush a small glass baking dish (just large enough to hold the 8 breasts comfortably) with butter and put the stuffed breasts into the baking dish. Brush the tops of the stuffed breasts liberally with the melted butter. Bake breasts until golden brown, about 30 to 35 minutes. Don't overcook or the chicken will be dry. Serves 8.

Curried Slippery Chicken
with Red Chile Peanut Sauce

This Asian-inspired curry dish is easy to prepare a day ahead and put together at the last minute. Serve it with a chilly, fresh salad and lots of cold drinks!

2 cups unsweetened coconut milk
1 Tbs. soy sauce
2 tsp. curry powder
1 tsp. coriander seeds, toasted
    and ground
1/2 Tbs. dry sherry
5 Tbs. corn or peanut oil
2 tsp. cornstarch
2 whole skinless, boneless
    chicken breasts

1 Tbs. ginger, finely diced
3 scallions (including greens), finely
    diced
1 large garlic clove, finely diced
3/4 cup salted, roasted peanuts,
    finely ground
1 or 2 tsp. freshly squeezed
    lime juice
1 or 2 tsp. chile Caribe, to taste
2 Tbs. minced fresh cilantro leaves

Stir together the coconut milk, soy sauce, curry powder and ground coriander seeds. Put 1/2 cup of the coconut mixture into a medium bowl, and stir in the sherry, 1 tablespoon oil, and the cornstarch. Cover and chill the remaining coconut mixture. Trim the chicken breasts and slice them thin (1/8 inch thick) across the grain. Gently stir the chicken pieces into the cornstarch mixture to coat each piece, and marinate at least 1 hour and up to 24 hours.

Heat 6 cups of water to boiling in a large pot and add 1 tablespoon oil. Lower the heat to medium, scatter the chicken pieces in the water, and stir to separate. Simmer and stir gently until the chicken pieces turn white, about 1 minute; drain the chicken immediately in a strainer and set aside. (If you are going to finish the dish later, cover the chicken and refrigerate up to 24 hours.) Put the reserved coconut mixture, peanuts, lime juice, and chile Caribe in a small sauce pan and simmer 10 minutes, stirring, until just thickened. Remove from heat and keep warm.

Heat a wok or deep skillet until very hot. Swirl 1 tablespoon oil in the wok until hot, then scatter in the diced ginger, scallions, and garlic and stir-fry for about 30 to 45 seconds. Swirl in the remaining 2 tablespoons of oil for only about 30 seconds, then quickly scatter the chicken pieces into the wok and stir-fry (keep the chicken moving so the pieces don't stick to the pan) just until cooked through, about 1 minute. Remove the wok from the heat and pour the warm sauce over the chicken, stirring to coat. Serve immediately over lots of hot rice; sprinkle with cilantro leaves. For a company spread, scatter the table with pretty saucers of chopped peanuts, mango chutney, plump raisins, toasted coconut, diced banana or pineapple, or Red Chile Ginger Gremolata (page 22). Serves 6 to 8.

Red Chile Fried Chicken

1 whole broiling chicken, cut up
1 cup buttermilk
1 cup all-purpose flour
1/2 cup Panko or dry bread crumbs
1 Tbs. salt
1 tsp. coriander seeds, toasted
   and ground

1/2 tsp. dried Mexican oregano
1 tsp. Chimayó chile powder
1/4 tsp. freshly ground pepper
1 cup corn or other vegetable oil

Wash and dry the chicken pieces and put in a glass baking dish. Pour the buttermilk over the chicken and turn to coat. Cover the dish with plastic wrap and marinate in the refrigerator for 1 hour. Mix the flour with the bread crumbs, salt, and spices in a large plastic bag. One at a time, remove the chicken pieces from the buttermilk and drain, then drop into the seasoned flour and shake to coat thoroughly. Put the chicken pieces on a rack to dry. In a large, heavy skillet heat the oil until hot. Brown the chicken pieces on both sides, about 15 minutes; then reduce the heat, add 2 tablespoons of water and cover the skillet tightly. Continue cooking about 30 minutes (checking frequently to guard against scorching), then remove the cover. Continue frying the chicken another 10 or 15 minutes until coating is crispy and meat is cooked through. Serves 4.

Herbed Chimayó Smoked Chicken

This savory, marinated chicken should be slow cooked in a smoker or covered barbecue to fully absorb the flavors of the marinade and remain moist and succulent.

$^1/_2$ cup freshly squeezed lemon juice
$^1/_2$ cup freshly squeezed
    orange juice
$^1/_2$ cup white wine
$^1/_4$ cup olive oil
1 Tbs. Chimayó chile powder,
    or to taste
6 garlic cloves, chopped

1 small white onion, chopped
2 Tbs. honey
$^1/_4$ to $^1/_2$ cup fresh chopped herbs,
    such as oregano, chervil,
    and parsley
2 tsp. salt
4 whole chicken breasts, halved and
    boned, with skin

A day ahead, puree everything but the chicken in a blender. Put the chicken pieces in a glass dish, pour the herb mixture over the chicken, cover, and marinate in the refrigerator overnight, turning occasionally. When ready to cook, drain the chicken (reserving the marinade) and let stand a half hour at room temperature while you prepare the smoker or barbecue pit. Boil the reserved marinade in a small saucepan for 5 minutes, then remove from heat. Season the chicken with salt and pepper, then slow cook, brushing occasionally with reserved marinade, for 45 minutes to 1 hour until cooked through. Serves 8.

Chile-Glazed Roast Cornish Game Hens

These little hens can be marinated a day ahead and popped in a hot oven just before the guests arrive. If you're cooking outside, they do well on a grill provided they are covered after the skin is seared to help keep the juices in.

2 red jalapeños, seeded
  and minced
3 scallions, sliced thin
2 Tbs. fresh ginger, peeled
  and minced
1 clove garlic, minced
1 to 2 Tbs. fresh cilantro leaves,
  chopped
1 tsp.fresh lime zest

1 Tbs. Chimayó red chile powder
1/4 cup soy sauce
1/2 cup white wine
4 Tbs. vegetable oil
1 Tbs. turbinado or brown sugar
1/4 tsp. salt
4 Cornish game hens, cleaned
  and split

Blend all ingredients except the game hens in a food processor until thoroughly combined. Put the split hens in a glass dish just large enough to hold them (or a heavy-duty plastic freezer bag set on a platter) and pour the marinade over the hens, turning to coat. Marinate the hens in the refrigerator for at least 4 hours and up to 24 hours, turning several times.

Preheat the oven to 450 degrees and bring the hens to room temperature. Remove the hens from the marinade and arrange them on a rack in a baking pan, skin side up. Put the hens in the preheated oven, then turn the oven temperature down to 375 degrees and bake the hens about 30 minutes, or until juices run yellow. Meanwhile, boil the marinade in a small saucepan for 5 minutes and use to baste the hens 2 or 3 times during baking. Serve the hens on mounds of hot, fluffy rice garnished with chopped cilantro. Serves 8.

Chicken Albondigas

Serve these savory chicken balls over rice or creamy mashed potatoes. This tasty dish can be made from leftover chicken.

3 cups cooked chicken, chopped
2 cloves garlic
2 slices French bread, soaked in
    milk and squeezed dry
2 tomatoes, peeled, seeded,
    and chopped
2 Tbs. fresh parsley leaves
1 tsp. dried oregano
1/8 tsp. ground cloves
2 tsp. New Mexico red
    chile powder

1 egg, beaten
2 quarts boiling chicken
    or vegetable stock
1/4 cup unsalted butter, softened
3/4 cup blanched and skinned
    almonds, ground
Salt and freshly ground pepper,
    to taste
Dash of hot red chile sauce,
    to taste

Put the chicken in a food processor with the garlic, bread, tomatoes and parsley and process to a smooth mixture. Scrape the chicken mixture into a medium bowl and sprinkle with oregano, cloves, and chile powder. Beat the egg into the chicken mixture until thoroughly combined. Roll chicken balls about the size of a walnut and set them on a plate to dry. In a heavy pot, bring the stock to a rolling boil and add the butter. Drop the albondigas into the stock and cook at a gentle boil until done, about 20 to 30 minutes. Remove the albondigas with a slotted spoon, and boil the broth down by almost half. Stir the ground almonds into the broth and cook until slightly thickened. Taste the sauce for seasoning and add salt and pepper, and red chile sauce to taste. Return the albondigas to the sauce to heat through. Serves 4 to 6.

Meats

Audrey's Chile Barbecue Brisket

This slow-cooked brisket is simple to prepare, though your guests may imagine you have slaved for many hours to produce it. Use New Mexico Red Barbecue Sauce (page 30), make your own favorite barbecue sauce, or use a good bottled brand.

2 cups barbecue sauce
1/2 cup Worcestershire Sauce
1/2 cup red wine vinegar
1/4 cup honey

2 tsp. red chile powder, or to taste
4 to 6 garlic cloves
6 to 8 lbs. beef brisket

Thoroughly combine all ingredients except the brisket. Pour the sauce over the brisket in a glass or enamel roasting pan just large enough to hold the meat, cover tightly with foil, and refrigerate overnight, turning occasionally. Set the oven at 200 degrees and cook the brisket, covered, for 12 to 14 hours. Serves 10 to 12.

❜ ❜ ❜

Chile Blue Cheese Crusted Steak

An elegant and unusual treatment for filet mignon, these steaks are quick to prepare and make an elegant presentation surrounded by garlic mashed potatoes and grilled mushroom caps.

8 oz. unsalted butter, softened
5 oz. blue cheese
1/2 cup fresh bread crumbs
1 tsp. Chimayó red chile powder, or
   to taste

1/4 tsp. freshly ground black pepper
4 filet mignon steaks, about
   8 oz. each

Mix the softened butter with the cheese, bread crumbs, chile powder, and pepper, roll into a log shape, wrap in wax paper, and chill. Grill or sauté the steaks to medium rare and arrange on a heat-proof platter. Top each steak with 1/4 of the chilled butter mixture and slide the platter under the broiler 3 to 4 inches from the flame until the tops of the steaks are golden brown and crusted. Serves 4.

Rib Eye Steak with Wild Mushrooms

1 tsp. salt
1 tsp. freshly ground black pepper
1 tsp. Chimayó chile powder
2 cloves garlic, minced
2 thick, bone-in rib eye steaks
   (1 1/2 to 2 lbs.)
1 Tbs. olive oil
2 slices bacon, chopped
1/2 medium white onion, chopped

1/2 lb. fresh mushrooms (shiitake,
   crimoni, or portabello)
1 tsp. chile Caribe
1 cup chicken broth
3 garlic cloves, minced
2 Tbs. parsley leaves, chopped
1 Tbs. freshly squeezed lime juice
Salt and freshly ground pepper,
   to taste

Preheat the oven to 350 degrees. Mix the salt, pepper, chile powder, and garlic together and rub the steaks thoroughly with the mixture; refrigerate for up to 4 hours. Bring the steaks to room temperature before proceeding. Heat 1 tablespoon oil in a heavy skillet, sear the steaks about 3 minutes on each side and transfer to a rack set in roasting pan. Roast the steaks 20 to 25 minutes, remove from oven and let stand (covered) for 10 minutes. Meanwhile, sauté the bacon and onion over high heat until golden. Stir in the mushrooms and chile Caribe and reduce heat. Continue to sauté gently until mushrooms are cooked and the liquid has evaporated. Add the broth to the mushrooms and boil until liquid is reduced by half. Add the minced garlic and parsley, the lime juice and the steak juices, and simmer a few minutes until slightly thickened. Taste for seasoning and add salt and pepper to taste. Pass the sauce with the steaks. Serves 2.

Grilled Steak with Guajillo Chile Sauce

This sauce would also be good with roasted pork or lamb.

6 cloves garlic
12 to 16 guajillo chiles,
   stemmed and seeded
2 Tbs. lard or vegetable oil
1 tsp. Mexican oregano
1/4 tsp. freshly ground pepper
1/8 tsp. cumin, toasted and ground

3 cups beef broth
1 tsp. honey
Salt and freshly ground pepper,
   to taste
6 New York strip steaks, about
   1-inch thick
6 Tbs. cilantro leaves, chopped

Roast the unpeeled garlic, wrapped in foil, in a 400-degree oven for 20 minutes; cool and peel. Wipe the dried chiles with a damp cloth, discard the stems and seeds, and tear into pieces. Heat the lard or oil in a heavy saucepan and fry the chiles in the hot oil until fragrant, about 5 minutes, stirring to prevent scorching. Remove them to a bowl and cover with boiling water, allow to soften, 20 or 30 minutes. Put the chiles in a blender with about a cup of the soaking water and the garlic, oregano, pepper, and cumin and blend to a puree. Reheat the oil in which the chiles were fried, and pour the puree into the hot oil. Sauté the puree, stirring constantly, about 5 minutes. Stir in the beef broth and honey and simmer the sauce over a low flame 45 minutes to an hour. Taste for seasoning and add salt and pepper if you like. Prepare the grill or broiler, and cook the steaks to medium rare. Brush with guajillo sauce and continue to grill or broil until done to your liking. Drizzle the steaks with guajillo sauce and sprinkle with chopped cilantro. Pass additional sauce on the side. Serves 6.

Chipotle Flank Steak

The marinade will tenderize the flank steak. Serve the steak with an array of cooling garnishes such as shredded lettuce, diced fresh tomato, chopped cilantro, diced avocado, sliced radishes, and sour cream.

1 head garlic, cloves separated
6 ancho chiles
2 mulato chiles
6 chipotle chiles
1 Tbs. vegetable oil
1 large orange, peeled and
  sectioned, with all pith removed
1/4 tsp. ground cinnamon

1/8 tsp. ground cloves
1/2 tsp. cumin seeds, toasted
  and ground
1 tsp. Mexican oregano
2 Tbs. cider vinegar
2 Tbs. honey
Salt, to taste
4 lbs. flank steak

Preheat the oven to 400 degrees. Wrap the garlic cloves in a "packet" of aluminum foil and roast in the hot oven about 20 minutes; cool the garlic and peel the skins. Wipe the dried chiles with a damp cloth, discard the stems and seeds, and tear into pieces. Heat the oil in a heavy skillet and fry the chiles in the hot oil until fragrant (about 5 minutes), stirring to prevent scorching. Remove them to a bowl and cover with boiling water, allow to soften (20 or 30 minutes). Put the garlic and chiles in a blender with remaining ingredients (except for the steaks) and blend to a thick puree. Rub the puree on the steaks and refrigerate for 2 to 4 hours, turning occasionally. Grill or roast the steaks to desired doneness, and slice across the grain. Serves 6 to 8.

High Plains Meatballs

This is a good way to prepare less tender cuts of venison or buffalo, but beef will do as well. Serve the meatballs in your favorite red chile sauce, barbecue sauce, or a sauce of sour cream mixed with yogurt and seasoned with freshly ground cumin, chile Caribe, and fresh minced scallions. You can brown the meatballs for freezer storage, adding the sauces when you serve them.

1 lb. finely ground venison or
    buffalo meat
1/2 medium white onion, minced
2 thick slices sourdough bread,
    soaked in milk and squeezed out
2 Tbs. pasilla chile puree
    (see page 16)

1 egg, lightly beaten
1 tsp. Mexican oregano
1 tsp. salt
1/4 tsp. freshly ground black pepper
2 or 3 Tbs. good olive oil

Thoroughly combine the ground meat, onion, soaked bread, chile puree, egg, oregano, salt and pepper and beat with a wooden spoon to a uniform light texture. Form the meat mixture into walnut-size balls and brown them in hot oil in a heavy skillet, shaking the skillet to keep the meatballs rolling. After they have browned, cover the skillet, reduce the heat a little and cook the meatballs until done, about 10 minutes. Serves 4.

Ancho Apricot Glazed Pork Chops

The flavors of ancho and apricot are a wonderful complement. You can substitute 2/3 cup of apricot preserves for the dried apricots (and omit the sugar in the glaze).

1/2 Tbs. olive oil
1/2 small white onion, finely minced
1 clove garlic, minced
2 Tbs. brown sugar
2 Tbs. dark soy sauce
4 Tbs. ancho chile puree
    (see page 16)

1/3 cup dry white wine
2/3 cup water
4 oz. dried apricots, finely chopped
4 thick pork loin chops
    (about 1 1/2 lbs.)
Salt and freshly ground pepper,
    to taste

Heat oil in a heavy, enameled saucepan and sauté onion until translucent. Add garlic and cook about 1 minute. Add brown sugar, soy sauce, chile puree, wine, water, and apricots and bring to a simmer. Cook on low heat, stirring until the mixture is thick and the apricots are soft, 20 to 30 minutes. Season the pork chops with salt and pepper.

Pour 1/2 the glaze over the pork chops in a small glass dish, and marinate in refrigerator for 2 to 4 hours. Preheat the oven broiler, setting the rack about 7 inches below the flame. Broil the chops 8 minutes on each side, turning once, until done. Meanwhile, warm the remaining glaze over a low flame. Serve the pork chops with remaining chile apricot glaze on the side. Serves 4.

Pork with Chile Colorado

This typical New Mexico pork dish is simple to make and freezes well.

3 Tbs. lard or vegetable oil
1 1/2 lbs. boned pork shoulder, cut
   into 1-inch chunks
4 New Mexico red chiles
2 large cloves garlic
1 tsp. cumin seeds, toasted
   and ground

1 tsp. Mexican oregano
1/2 tsp. ground cinnamon
1/2 tsp. salt
2 cups rich chicken stock

Heat the oil in a large, heavy pot and brown the pork in batches over high heat. Remove to a plate. Wipe the dried chiles with a damp cloth, discard the stems and seeds, and tear into pieces. Fry the chiles in the hot oil until fragrant (about 5 minutes), stirring to prevent scorching. Remove them to a bowl, cover with boiling water, and allow to soften (20 or 30 minutes). Put the chiles in a blender with about 1/2 cup of the soaking water and the garlic, cumin, oregano, cinnamon, and salt. Blend to a puree. Reheat the oil in the pot, and pour the puree into the hot oil. Sauté the puree, stirring constantly, about 5 minutes. Stir the stock into the puree, then return the pork to the pot. Bring the stew to a boil, cover, reduce heat, and stew the meat slowly for about an hour. Remove the cover and continue simmering 30 minutes to an hour until the pork is very tender. Add more chicken stock, if necessary, to keep the meat moist. Serves 4.

Whiskey-Glazed Chile Ribs

These barbecued ribs get a lot of their smoky flavor from using real hickory chips, which you can often find at stores that sell grilling equipment or at your local supermarket.

2 Tbs. brown sugar
2 tsp. Chimayó chile powder
1/4 tsp. salt
1/4 tsp. celery seeds
1/4 tsp. freshly ground black pepper
1 garlic clove, minced
5 lbs. of trimmed pork spare ribs
5 cups hickory wood chips
1/2 cup bourbon whiskey

1/2 cup catsup
2 Tbs. ancho or pasilla chile puree
   (see page 16)
1/4 cup dark molasses
1/4 cup soy sauce
1/4 cup olive oil
2 tsp. 3-pepper or other
   hot pepper sauce
1/2 cup beer

Mix together the brown sugar, chile powder, salt, celery seed, pepper, and garlic and rub the ribs all over with the mix; chill the ribs, covered, for 3 to 4 hours. Meanwhile, soak the hickory wood chips in cold water for 3 hours; then drain thoroughly.

In a heavy saucepan, simmer the whiskey, catsup, chile puree, molasses, soy sauce, and olive oil over moderate heat about 5 minutes. Taste for seasoning, and add salt and pepper to taste. Cool the glaze to room temperature. Prepare the grill by arranging coals around a foil drip pan placed under the center of the grill rack to catch meat juices. When the coals turn gray with ash, spread the drained hickory wood chips over the coals. Cut the ribs into serving pieces and arrange them in one layer on an oiled rack about 6 inches above the drip pan and close the grill lid. Cook the ribs about an hour, turning occasionally, until browned but not burned. During the last 15 minutes on the grill, brush the ribs with whiskey glaze. Meanwhile, preheat the oven to 350 degrees. When the ribs are browned, remove them to a roasting pan, pour the whiskey glaze, the beer and the pan drippings from the grill over them and bake about 30 minutes to finish cooking. Serves 4 to 6.

Christmas Ham

Santa Fe "Christmas" style ham uses both red and green chiles in a piquant cherry chile glaze that doubles as a rich table sauce.

6 to 8 lb. half ham, bone in
12 oz. frozen pitted cherries,
 thawed
1¹/2 cups red chile honey
3 Tbs. freshly squeezed lime juice

2 tsp. lime zest
1 fresh green jalapeño chile,
 seeded and minced
3 Tbs. fresh cilantro leaves,
 chopped

Preheat the oven to 325 degrees. Place the ham, fat side up, on a rack in a roasting pan. Bake a total of 3 to 3¹/2 hours, or to internal temperature of 160 degrees. Meanwhile, thaw cherries and drain, reserving juice. Set aside half the cherries, and mince the remainder. In a medium saucepan, bring the honey, lime juice, lime zest, jalapeño chile, 2 tablespoons cilantro, minced cherries, and reserved cherry juice to a simmer over low heat, stirring to combine thoroughly. Remove from heat and set aside.

About 30 minutes before the ham is done, remove from the oven and pour off the drippings, reserving pan juices. Score the ham fat, cutting about ¹/4 inch deep, and spoon some of the cherry chile glaze over the ham. Return to the oven and continue roasting, spooning more glaze over the ham about every 7 minutes or so. Remove the ham from the oven and let stand, covered, about 15 minutes while you make the sauce. Pour the fat off the reserved ham roasting juices or remove with a bulb baster. Pour about ¹/2 cup of the ham roasting juices (or to taste) into the remaining cherry chile glaze, add the reserved whole cherries, and bring to a simmer, stirring to combine. Carve the ham and garnish with the remaining chopped cilantro leaves. Serve with warm cherry chile sauce on the side. Serves 12.

Ancho Chile Glazed Lamb Shanks

The shanks can be cooked a day ahead and refrigerated, then baked in their chile glaze just before the guests arrive. Be sure to bring them to room temperature before baking, or they won't heat through before the glaze begins to scorch.

1/4 cup good olive oil
4 lamb shanks
Salt and freshly ground pepper,
    to taste
1 onion, finely chopped
2 large cloves garlic, minced
4 large tomatoes, peeled, seeded,
    and diced
1 stalk celery, sliced
2 cups rich chicken stock or
    vegetable broth
2 ancho chiles, rinsed, stemmed,
    and seeded
1 tsp. cumin seed, toasted
    and ground

4 whole peppercorns
1 bay leaf
3 Tbs. ancho chile puree,
    (see page 16)
1/2 cup honey
1/3 cup freshly squeezed
    orange juice
Salt and freshly ground pepper
    to taste
2 Tbs. mint or cilantro leaves,
    chopped
1/2 cup Red Chile Ginger
    Gremolata (page 22)

Preheat the oven to 350 degrees. Heat the oil in a large, heavy pot until hot, but not smoking. Season the shanks with salt and pepper and brown on all sides in the hot oil, about 8 minutes. Transfer the shanks to a plate. In the oil remaining in the pot, sauté the onion for 3 minutes; add the garlic and sauté another 2 minutes. Stir in the tomatoes, celery, stock, ancho chiles, cumin, peppercorns, and bay leaf. Return the lamb to the pot, bring to a boil, cover, and cook in the oven 1 1/2 to 2 hours until the shanks are tender. Remove the shanks to a very shallow baking pan; strain and reserve the lamb cooking liquid in a medium saucepan.

Turn the oven up to 400 degrees. Mix ancho puree, honey, and orange juice in a small saucepan and bring to a boil, stirring. Simmer the reserved lamb cooking liquid until slightly thickened and reduced to about 1 cup. Pour about 1/2 cup of the honey mixture into the reduced lamb cooking liquid, check for seasoning and add salt and pepper to taste, and keep warm. Brush the lamb with the remaining honey mixture and bake in the hot oven until the shanks are nicely glazed, about 10 to 20 minutes. Serve shanks sprinkled with chopped mint or cilantro and Red Chile Ginger Gremolata. Pour out the sauce from the baking pan and pass separately. Serves 4.

Pasta, Beans, and Rice

Red Macaroni and Cheese

2 cups elbow macaroni
1¹/₂ tsp. salt
1 Tbs. Chimayó chile powder
¹/₄ tsp. cumin seed, toasted
   and ground
¹/₄ tsp. ground cinnamon
¹/₈ tsp. freshly grated nutmeg
³/₄ cup sour cream
2¹/₄ cups whole milk
¹/₂ cup heavy cream

1¹/₂ Tbs. unsalted butter
2 Tbs. all-purpose flour
1¹/₄ cups Monterey Jack cheese,
   shredded
2 large eggs, beaten
Dash of red chile hot sauce,
   to taste
1¹/₄ cups sharp cheddar cheese,
   grated

Preheat the oven to 350 degrees, and butter a 3-quart glass baking dish. In a large pot, cook the macaroni in several quarts of boiling salted water until just al dente. Drain the macaroni thoroughly, and set aside in the buttered baking dish, covered. In a small bowl, whisk the salt, chile powder, cumin, cinnamon, and nutmeg into the sour cream and set aside.

In a small saucepan, bring the milk and cream to a simmer, and cut off the heat. In a heavy, enameled saucepan, melt the butter over medium-high heat and whisk in the flour. Cook the roux, whisking constantly, for 3 minutes, but do not allow to brown. Pour in the hot milk mixture, whisking constantly; reduce the heat to low and cook the sauce for 2 minutes. Stir in the seasoned sour cream mixture, the shredded Monterey Jack cheese, and the eggs until well blended. Season the sauce with hot red chile sauce to taste, and pour it over the macaroni in the baking dish, stirring to mix. Sprinkle the top of the casserole with grated cheddar cheese and bake 25 to 30 minutes, until hot through and nicely browned on top. Let stand 10 minutes before serving. Serves 8 to 10.

Linguine with Ancho Gorgonzola Sauce

1 lb. linguine
2 Tbs. extra-virgin olive oil
2 shallots, sliced
1 clove garlic, minced
1 medium, ripe tomato, peeled,
    seeded, and diced
Salt and freshly ground pepper,
    to taste

1 Tbs. ancho chile puree
    (see page 16)
1/2 cup rich chicken or vegetable
    stock
1/2 cup heavy cream
4 to 6 oz. gorgonzola or other
    blue cheese
2 Tbs. parsley, minced

In a large pot, cook the linguine in several quarts of boiling salted water until just al dente. Drain, return it to its cooking pot, cover, and set aside to keep warm. Heat the olive oil in a large, heavy skillet and sauté the shallots on medium-high heat for about 2 minutes. Add the minced garlic and cook another minute. Stir in the diced tomatoes, season with salt and pepper, and cook 5 minutes, or until most of the tomato liquid has evaporated. Stir in the chile puree; add the stock and cream and cook, stirring, until the sauce is creamy and well blended, about 5 minutes. Just before serving, stir the gorgonzola into the hot sauce and stir until it begins to melt. Pour the sauce over the reserved linguine and toss to mix. Serve immediately, sprinkling each serving with minced parsley. Serves 4.

Chimayó Chicken and Penne Casserole

This creamy casserole freezes beautifully. We have made the recipe substituting fresh sea scallops for the chicken.

1 lb. penne pasta
2 large chicken breasts, boned
  and skinned
1 large red bell pepper, roasted,
  peeled, and seeded
2 Tbs. virgin olive oil
1/4 cup fresh garlic, minced

1/4 cup fresh basil, chopped
3 tsp. Chimayó chile powder
1 cup dry white wine
1/2 cup light cream
1/2 cup Parmesan cheese,
  freshly grated

Preheat the oven to 350 degrees, and oil a medium baking dish. In a large pot, cook the penne in several quarts of boiling salted water until just al dente. Drain the penne thoroughly, and set aside in the oiled baking dish, covered. Wash and dry the chicken breasts, slice across the grain into julienne strips, and set aside. Cut the roasted bell pepper into julienne strips and set aside. In a large, heavy skillet, heat the olive oil and sauté the garlic and all but 1 tablespoon of the basil for about 2 minutes. Add the julienned chicken and toss quickly in the hot oil to brown, about 4 or 5 minutes. Sprinkle the chicken with chile powder, pour in the white wine, and simmer the mixture for 10 to 15 minutes. Stir in the cream and the roasted pepper strips and continue to simmer slowly until the liquid is reduced and thickened to a creamy sauce. Pour the sauce over the cooked penne in the baking dish and stir gently to mix. Sprinkle the grated Parmesan over the casserole and bake for 10 to 12 minutes. Let the dish stand 10 minutes, then sprinkle with the remaining basil and serve. Serves 4 to 6.

New Mexico Ranch Beans

Guaranteed to please serious chile addicts, these beans are even better a day or two after cooking. Serve with sour cream on the side, and lots of hot tortillas and cold beer.

1 lb. pinto beans
1 ham hock
1 small white onion, chopped
1 herb bouquet (2 sprigs parsley,
    2 unpeeled garlic cloves, 1 large
    bay leaf, 1 clove, and 2 sprigs
    fresh thyme tied in cheesecloth)
1 Tbs. salt
1 sprig epazote
1 very large, ripe tomato, peeled,
    seeded, and roughly chopped
1/2 medium white onion, roughly
    chopped

2 garlic cloves, peeled
2 or 3 dried New Mexico red chiles,
    stemmed, seeded,
    and soaked
1 dried chipotle chile, stemmed,
    seeded, and soaked
2 tsp. Mexican oregano
1 tsp. cumin seeds, toasted
    and slightly crushed
2 Tbs. lard or vegetable oil

Cover the beans with cold water in a large, heavy pot and soak them overnight; or bring to a boil, cut off the heat, and let stand 1 hour. Drain the beans and discard the water. Cover the soaked beans with fresh cold water, add the ham hock, chopped onion, and the herb bouquet. Bring to a simmer and cook uncovered until done, from 2 to 4 hours depending on the beans, adding water if necessary to keep them from drying out. Thirty minutes before the end of the cooking time, add the salt and epazote. When the beans are cooked tender but still firmly holding their shape, discard the herb bouquet and the epazote sprig, remove the ham hock, and set aside.

Put the tomato, onion, garlic, chiles, oregano, and cumin seed into a blender or food processor with a few tablespoons of bean cooking liquid and process to a thin puree. In a heavy skillet, heat the lard or oil until hot but not smoking, and pour the sauce carefully into the hot fat (it will spatter, so be careful). Cook the sauce, stirring constantly, for 3 or 4 minutes, being careful not to burn it. Stir the sauce into the beans and continue cooking the beans over low heat for 20 to 30 minutes to absorb flavor. Before serving, cut up the meat from the ham hock and stir it into the beans. Serves 6 to 8.

Borracho Baked Beans

Beans are often cooked with beer in central Mexico (*borracho* means "drunken"), but this recipe adds a molasses-baked technique from New England to yield a slightly sweet-hot dish, great with barbecued or grilled meats. Baked 1 day ahead, the beans are even better!

1/2 lb. bacon, chopped
1 large white onion, chopped
2 garlic cloves, minced
2 Tbs. Chimayó chile powder,
* or to taste*
3 Tbs. pasilla chile puree
* (see page 16)*
1 1/2 cups Mexican dark beer

1/4 cup dark molasses
1 Tbs. Mexican oregano
2 tsp. cumin seeds, toasted
* and crushed*
2 tsp. salt
1 lb. pinto beans (dry weight),
* cooked and drained,*
* reserving liquid*

Preheat the oven to 250 degrees. In a heavy skillet, sauté the bacon and onions over medium-low heat until the bacon has crisped and browned and the onions are wilted, about 7 minutes. Add the minced garlic to the skillet and cook 2 minutes, then set aside.

Put the drained beans into a bean pot or a 6- to 8-cup casserole dish with a lid. In a medium bowl, whisk the chile powder into the chile puree, then slowly whisk in 3/4 cup of the beer to make a smooth liquid. In a medium saucepan, bring the remaining beer to a boil. Whisk the chile mixture, molasses, oregano, cumin, and salt into the beer until thoroughly combined. Pour the boiling beer mixture over the beans, adding bean cooking liquid if necessary to bring the liquid just level with the top of the beans. Cover the casserole and bake for 5 to 6 hours, adding bean-cooking liquid from time to time, if necessary, to keep the beans from drying out. Serves 6 to 8.

Black Bean Refritos

As anyone from the Southwest will tell you, life without refried beans is not worth living. We mash the beans with fresh bacon fat to get the full, traditional richness of the dish. Vegetable oil is an alternative, though you will be sacrificing some depth of flavor. These are best made with beans home cooked with ham hock, herbs, and spices, but canned beans will do in a pinch. You can freeze the refritos—tightly wrapped, they will be good for up to 2 months.

1 lb. dry black beans
  (or 4 cups canned beans)
1/4 lb. fresh bacon (pork belly)
1 small white onion, halved
2 sprigs parsley
2 bay leaves
2 unpeeled garlic cloves
1 Tbs. salt
6 to 8 Tbs. fresh bacon fat,
  to taste
1 large white onion, minced
1/2 red bell pepper, minced

1 fresh red Fresno or red jalapeño
  chile, seeded and minced
4 cloves garlic, minced
2 large, ripe tomatoes, peeled,
  seeded, and chopped fine
1 tsp. Mexican oregano
2 Tbs. fresh cilantro, minced
Salt and freshly ground black
  pepper to taste
1/2 cup Manchego or feta cheese,
  crumbled

Soak the dry beans overnight in water to cover; drain and discard water. In a large, heavy pot, cover the beans with water and add the chunk of fresh bacon, onion, parsley, bay leaves, and garlic. Bring to a simmer and cook, uncovered, until done, from 2 to 4 hours depending on the beans. About 30 minutes before the end of cooking time, add 1 tablespoon of salt.

Drain cooked beans and set aside the cooking liquid. In a big, heavy skillet, heat 2 tablespoons of bacon fat and sauté the onion, red bell pepper, and minced chile over medium heat until the vegetables are wilted and there's a great aroma in the kitchen, about 5 to 7 minutes. Add the garlic and oregano and cook for 2 minutes; add the tomatoes and continue cooking until most of the liquid is evaporated, about 5 minutes. Scrape the mixture into a bowl and set aside.

Heat 2 tablespoons of bacon fat in the skillet and add 1/4 of the drained beans. Mash the beans with a wooden spoon, mixing with the fat and stirring in reserved bean cooking liquid by tablespoons to achieve your preferred consistency (we like it chunky, leaving lots of beans more or less intact). Continue adding bacon fat by tablespoons and more beans and liquid until all the beans have been incorporated. Stir in the tomato mixture and 1 tablespoon of cilantro, add salt and pepper to taste, and heat through. Serve the refritos hot, sprinkled with crumbled cheese and the remaining cilantro. Serves 6 to 8.

Black Bean Cakes

Serve these bean cakes hot with a dollop of sour cream and a good salsa fresca. You can make them up in batches and keep them on hand in the freezer for up to 1 month, then crisp in a hot oven. These are best made with beans you cooked yourself with ham hock, herbs, and spices, but canned beans will do in a pinch.

2 cups cooked, drained black beans
    (reserving liquid)
2 Tbs. mulato chile puree
    (see page 16)
2 Tbs. Chimayó chile powder
3 tsp. cumin seed, toasted
    and crushed

1/2 cup scallion, finely minced
1 Tbs. fresh oregano, minced
2 beaten eggs
6 Tbs. flour
Salt and freshly ground pepper,
    to taste
Vegetable oil for frying

Lightly mash the drained beans as for refritos, leaving plenty of chunky texture. Stir in the chile puree, chile powder, cumin, scallion, and oregano and blend well. Beat in the eggs, then add the flour 1 tablespoon at a time. Season to taste with salt and pepper. If bean mixture seems too dry, add reserved bean liquid 1 tablespoon at a time to the consistency of a very thick batter. Heat about 1/4 inch of oil in a heavy skillet to hot but not smoking. Drop the bean mixture by heaping tablespoons into the hot oil and flatten out with a spatula into 3-inch cakes. Fry the bean cakes about 2 minutes on each side until they are crispy, and drain on paper towels. Serve the cakes hot. Serves 4 to 6.

Southwest Red Beans and Rice

This savory Cajun combination works well with a southwestern accent.

1 lb. pinto or red beans
1/4 lb. salt pork
1 small white onion, chopped
2 garlic cloves, minced
1 large carrot, finely diced
2 fresh red Fresno or
   jalapeño chiles, whole
1 Tbs. salt
2 cups long-grain rice

5 cups water
1 Tbs. olive oil
1 1/2 Tbs. salt
Salt and freshly ground pepper,
   to taste
1 cup sour cream
1/2 fresh red jalapeño chile,
   seeded and minced

Cover the beans with cold water in a large, heavy pot and soak them overnight; or bring to a boil, cut off the heat, and let stand 1 hour. Drain the beans and discard the water. Cover the soaked beans with fresh cold water, add the salt pork, chopped onion, minced garlic, chopped carrot, and whole chiles. Bring to a simmer and cook uncovered until done, from 2 to 4 hours depending on the beans, adding a little water if necessary to make sure plenty of liquid remains. Thirty minutes before the end of the cooking time, add 1 tablespoon salt. When the beans are cooked tender but still firmly holding their shape, remove the salt pork and the whole chiles and discard.

In a large, heavy saucepan bring the water, oil, and 1 1/2 tablespoons salt to a rolling boil. Sprinkle the rice into the water slowly to maintain a simmer, then cover the pan tightly, reduce the heat to low, and cook the rice until tender and all water is absorbed, about 20 minutes. Cut off the heat and keep rice covered and hot until ready to serve.

When ready to serve, fluff up the rice with a fork, season with salt and pepper, and spoon into deep plates or soup bowls. Spoon the red beans (and plenty of liquid) over the rice, add a dollop of sour cream, and sprinkle with a little minced jalapeño chile. Serves 8 to 10.

Spicy Spanish Rice

A lot of the flavor of this rich, spicy rice will depend on the quality of the stock, so try to use a good home-made broth.

2¹/2 cups rich chicken or
    vegetable stock
1 tsp. salt, or to taste
1 very large, ripe tomato, peeled,
    seeded, and roughly chopped
¹/2 medium white onion,
    roughly chopped
1 garlic clove, peeled

2 Tbs. ancho or pasilla chile puree
    (see page 16)
4 oz. chorizo sausage (optional)
3 to 4 Tbs. canola oil
1 cup long-grain rice
2 Tbs. fresh cilantro leaves,
    chopped

Bring the stock and salt to a simmer in a medium saucepan; lower the heat and keep the stock hot. Put the tomato, onion, garlic, chile puree, and a few tablespoons of the stock into a blender or food processor and blend to a puree. Remove the chorizo sausage from its casing, and fry in a small skillet until browned, breaking up the meat with a fork. Drain the cooked chorizo on paper toweling and set aside.

In a large, heavy saucepan with a close-fitting lid, heat the oil over medium-high heat and stir the rice into the hot oil. Sauté the rice in the oil, stirring constantly, until it is translucent and golden, about 8 minutes. Scrape the tomato-chile puree into the saucepan with the rice and cook, stirring, for 3 or 4 minutes. Do not let the rice scorch. Pour the hot stock into the rice, quickly stir in the chorizo, cover the saucepan and cut the heat to low. Cook the rice for about 20 minutes, or until the rice grains are tender and the liquid has been absorbed. Sprinkle each serving with chopped cilantro. Serves 4.

Spicy Pasilla Risotto
with Roasted Red Pepper

2 to 3 Tbs. pasilla chile puree
  (see page 16)
4 cups chicken or vegetable stock
1/2 tsp. salt
3 Tbs. olive oil
1 red bell pepper, seeded and cut in
  julienne strips

1 onion minced
2 garlic cloves, minced
1 cup short-grain rice
1/3 cup white wine
1/4 cup Asiago cheese, grated
1 Tbs. fresh parsley, minced

In a medium saucepan, whisk a little stock into the chile puree to thin it, then pour in the remaining stock and the salt. Bring the stock mixture to a simmer, then lower the heat and keep the stock hot. In a large, heavy saucepan or deep skillet, heat the oil over medium-high heat and sauté the red pepper strips until softened and beginning to brown, then remove to a small bowl and set aside. Add the onion to the skillet and sauté until softened and translucent, about 6 minutes. Add the minced garlic and sauté 1 minute. Stir the rice into the onions and sauté, stirring constantly, about 3 minutes. Add 1/2 cup of the hot stock and cook, stirring, until the liquid is absorbed, about 5 minutes. Continue to add stock to the rice 1/2 cup at a time, stirring and cooking until the liquid is absorbed before adding the next 1/2 cup. When the last of the stock has been added, cook until the dish is creamy and the rice is cooked through. Stir in the peppers, cheese, and parsley, and serve immediately. Serves 6 to 8.

Ancho Rice Pilaf

This dish will have a mild heat, and the grains of rice will absorb the earthy, deep flavor of anchos. A wonderful side dish with seafood of any kind, this pilaf also complements chicken or turkey. It is best to use your own home-made chicken or vegetable broth.

1 medium onion, chopped fine
2 Tbs. olive oil
2 garlic cloves, minced
1 roasted red bell pepper, peeled,
    seeded, and chopped
1 fresh red jalapeño chile,
    seeded and minced
1 cup long-grain rice

3 Tbs. ancho chile puree
    (see page 16)
1½ cups rich chicken or
    vegetable broth
Salt and freshly ground
    black pepper, to taste
1 large scallion, sliced

In a large, deep skillet with a cover, sauté the onions in oil over medium-low heat until they are soft and translucent, about 8 minutes. Stir the minced garlic into the onions and cook 1 minute more. Add the chopped red pepper, minced chile, and rice, and cook over medium heat, stirring, until all the rice is coated with oil and has turned translucent, 3 to 4 minutes (do not burn the rice!). Stir in the chile puree, the heated broth, and salt and pepper to taste, and cover the skillet with a tight lid. Turn the heat to low, and cook the rice about 20 minutes, or until the liquid is absorbed and the rice is cooked through. When ready to serve, fluff the rice with a fork and stir in the scallions. Serves 4.

Breads

Blue Corn Muffins with Chile-Spiced Pecans

A southwestern staple for tortillas and breads, blue cornmeal has a special, nutty flavor when baked. For sweeter muffins, add another 1/3 cup of sugar.

1 Tbs. unsalted butter
1 cup fresh or frozen corn kernels
1 1/2 cups blue cornmeal
1 1/2 cups all-purpose flour
1 tsp. salt
1 tsp. baking soda
1 tsp. baking powder
2/3 cup turbinado sugar (or 1/3 cup
   each brown sugar and granulated
   sugar)

3/4 cup Chile-Spiced Nuts (pecans)
   (page 33), chopped
3 large eggs, separated, at room
   temperature
2 cups buttermilk
1/2 cup unsalted butter,
   melted and slightly cooled

Preheat the oven to 375 degrees. Butter a 12-muffin tin, or line with paper cups. In medium cast iron skillet, cook the corn kernels in the butter over medium heat, stirring, until browned and dry, about 6 minutes, and set aside. In a large mixing bowl, whisk together the corn meal, flour, salt, baking soda, baking powder, sugar, and spiced pecans. In another bowl, whisk the egg yolks with the buttermilk and melted butter. Beat the egg whites until stiff and glossy. Pour the milk mixture into the dry ingredients and stir just to combine. Stir in the pecans, and gently fold in the beaten egg whites. Spoon the batter into prepared muffin tins and bake 20 to 25 minutes. Makes 1 dozen muffins.

Chile Pita Crisps

6 rounds of pita bread,
   6-inch diameter
1/2 cup virgin olive oil
4 Tbs. grated fresh orange rind

2 tsp. Chimayó chile powder
1/4 cup fresh cilantro leaves, minced
Kosher salt to sprinkle

Preheat the oven to 350 degrees. Split the pita breads open cross-wise into two rounds, then cut each round into quarters. Using a pastry brush, coat the inside surface of each pita wedge with olive oil and arrange, oil side up, on a large baking sheet. In a small bowl, toss together the orange zest, chile powder, and minced cilantro leaves until well combined, and sprinkle the mixture evenly over the pita wedges. Sprinkle the wedges with coarse salt to taste, and bake until crisp, fragrant, and golden brown, about 3 to 5 minutes. Makes 48 crisps.

Chile-Spiced Pumpkin Bread

This rich, dark bread is easy to make and freezes beautifully.

1 medium red onion, very finely
   chopped
2 Tbs. unsalted butter
2 tsp. Chimayó chile powder
2 tsp. cumin seeds, toasted
   and ground
1/8 tsp. ground cloves
1/8 tsp. freshly grated nutmeg
1 1/2 cups all-purpose flour
1 1/2 cups yellow cornmeal

1 tsp. salt
1 tsp. baking soda
2 tsp. baking powder
2 Tbs. brown sugar
3 large eggs
3/4 cup buttermilk
6 Tbs. unsalted butter, melted
   and slightly cooled
2 cups fresh pumpkin puree
1 Tbs. fresh ginger, minced

Preheat the oven to 350 degrees and butter 2 loaf pans. In a heavy skillet, sauté the onion in butter until soft, about 6 minutes. Sprinkle the chile powder, 1 teaspoon cumin, the cloves, and nutmeg over the onions and sauté, stirring for 1 minute. Remove from heat and set aside. In a medium bowl, whisk together the flour, cornmeal, salt, baking soda, baking powder, and sugar. In a large mixing bowl, beat the eggs, buttermilk, and melted butter into the pumpkin puree until well combined. Stir in the ginger and remaining cumin seeds. Add the flour mixture and stir until the batter is just combined. Divide the batter between the prepared loaf pans and bake 45 to 50 minutes. Turn the loaves out on a rack to cool. Makes 2 loaves.

Jalapeño Cheese Corn Biscuits

These creamy corn biscuits can be eaten hot from the oven or split and toasted the next day.

1/2 small white onion, minced
2 fresh red jalapeño chiles,
* seeded and minced*
2 Tbs. unsalted butter
3/4 cup fresh or frozen corn kernels
2 cups all-purpose flour
1 cup yellow cornmeal
3/4 tsp. salt

2 Tbs. baking powder
1/2 tsp. Chimayó chile powder
3 Tbs. sugar
1/2 cup unsalted butter,
* cut in pieces*
1 cup mild cheddar cheese, shredded
1 1/4 cups light cream

Preheat the oven to 400 degrees. In a medium cast iron skillet, sauté the minced onion and jalapeño chile in butter over medium heat 3 minutes. Add the corn kernels to the skillet and cook until the corn begins to brown and the mixture is dry. Remove from heat and set aside. In a large mixing bowl, whisk together the flour, cornmeal, salt, baking powder, chile powder, and sugar. Cut the cold butter into the flour mixture until it is the consistency of coarse meal. Stir in the onion and corn mixture and the cheese; then pour in the cream and stir until just combined. Turn out on a well-floured board, knead a few times to combine, and roll or pat out gently to about 1 1/2 inch thick. Cut out biscuits with a floured cutter and arrange 1 inch apart on a baking sheet. Gather the scraps and roll out again to cut additional biscuits. Bake the biscuits 12 to 15 minutes, until nicely browned. Makes about 3 dozen biscuits.

Red Chile Scallion Dropped Biscuits

These are the easiest biscuits we've ever made—30 minutes start to finish.

2 cups all-purpose flour
1/2 tsp. salt
2 tsp. baking powder
1/4 tsp. baking soda
1 tsp. Chimayó chile powder
3 Tbs. unsalted butter,
   cut in pieces

1/4 cup scallions, minced
1 fresh red jalapeño chile,
   seeded and minced
1 cup buttermilk

Preheat the oven to 400 degrees. In a large mixing bowl, whisk together the flour, salt, baking powder, baking soda, and chile powder. Cut in the chilled butter until the mixture is crumbly, then stir in the scallions and minced fresh chile. Add the buttermilk, stirring just until the batter is moist. Drop the batter onto a greased cookie sheet by heaping tablespoons, and bake about 15 minutes, or until lightly browned. Makes 16 biscuits.

Red Chile Cumin Wafers

These rich, nutty nibbles are very easy to make, and the dough freezes beautifully.

1/2 lb. sharp cheddar cheese,
   shredded
3/4 cup unsalted butter, softened
4 tsp. cumin seed, toasted
   and lightly crushed
1 tsp. Chimayó chile powder

1/4 tsp. salt
1 dash of cayenne pepper
1/2 cup Chile-Spiced Nuts
   (page 33), coarsely ground
1 1/2 cups all purpose flour
1 egg, beaten with 1 Tbs. water

In a large mixing bowl, beat the shredded cheese into the softened butter with a wooden spoon. Sprinkle the crushed cumin seed, chile powder, salt, cayenne, and half the nuts over the mixture and beat again. Add all the flour and mix and knead it into the butter and cheese mixture until thoroughly combined. Divide the dough in half and roll each half into a log about 1 1/2 inches in diameter. Wrap the logs tightly in plastic wrap and chill for 2 hours.

Preheat the oven to 450 degrees. With a sharp knife, slice the logs into 1/8-inch-thick rounds and arrange on baking sheets. Using a pastry brush, coat the top of each wafer with egg wash and sprinkle with the remaining nuts. Bake the wafers 8 to 10 minutes until lightly browned. Remove from the oven and cool on a rack. Makes about 30 wafers.

Red Chile Blue Cheese Focaccia

2³/4 cups all purpose flour
1¹/2 tsp. active dry yeast
1 tsp. sugar
1 tsp. salt
3 tsp. fresh rosemary leaves,
    chopped, or 2 tsp. dried
¹/2 tsp. cumin seeds, lightly crushed
³/4 cup very warm water
¹/4 cup virgin olive oil

³/4 cup Chile Spiced Nuts (walnuts)
    (page 33), chopped
1 small red onion, very thin sliced
1 small red bell pepper, roasted,
    peeled, seeded, and sliced in thin
    strips
2 Tbs. unsalted butter, melted
1 cup crumbled blue cheese
1 tsp. Chimayó chile powder

With a balloon whisk, stir together the flour, yeast, sugar, salt, rosemary, and cumin. Add the very warm water, drizzling it evenly over the surface of the flour mixture. Let stand without stirring for about 10 minutes. Add the oil and spiced nuts, turn out onto a lightly floured board, and knead for 3 or 4 minutes. Shape the dough into a ball, place it in an oiled bowl, and turn over once to coat with oil. Cover with a cloth and let stand in a warm place to rise, about an hour.

Lightly punch down the dough, shape it into a ball, and place on a greased baking sheet. Press the dough down gently into a flat 12-inch circle and "dimple" it with your fingers. Arrange the onion rings and roasted red pepper strips on top and drizzle with melted butter. Toss the crumbled blue cheese with the chile powder, and sprinkle over the top of the focaccia. Set the dough in a warm place to rise another 30 minutes. Preheat the oven to 400 degrees. Bake the focaccia for 30 minutes, until nicely browned on top and crusty on the bottom. Cool on a rack 3 minutes, then cut in wedges and serve warm. Serves 12 to 16.

Red Chile Potato Bread

This flavored flat bread is best served straight from the oven.

1 large baking potato (about $^1/_2$ lb.),
    scrubbed
1 tsp. salt
2 tsp. active dry yeast
$^1/_4$ cup whole milk,
    at room temperature
$^1/_2$ tsp. sugar
$1^1/_2$ cups all-purpose flour
1 tsp. salt

1 large egg, beaten
2 Tbs. unsalted butter, softened
1 cup sun-dried tomatoes in oil
2 tsp. Chimayó chile powder
2 Tbs. chopped fresh cilantro,
    or 1 Tbs. dried
1 Tbs. virgin olive oil
Kosher salt for sprinkling

In a medium saucepan, cover the potato with cold water, add the salt, and bring to a boil. Reduce the heat and simmer until the potato is very tender, about 30 minutes. Drain the potato, reserving $^1/_4$ cup of cooking water in a medium bowl. When the potato is cool enough to handle, peel it, and pass through a ricer or mash thoroughly, and set aside to cool. Stir the yeast, milk, and sugar into the potato water and let proof until foamed, about 5 minutes. In a large bowl, whisk together the flour and salt. Beat the yeast mixture into the cooled potato, then beat in the egg and the softened butter. Scrape the potato mixture into the flour and salt, and beat until smooth. Cover the bowl and let stand in a warm place to rise about 1 hour. Punch down the dough, cover, and chill for 4 hours.

Shape the cold dough into a ball and place on a greased baking sheet. Press the dough down gently into a flat 12-inch circle and "dimple" it with your fingers. Sprinkle the tomatoes, chile powder, and cilantro evenly over the dough, then drizzle with olive oil and sprinkle with coarse salt to taste. Set in a warm place to rise for 30 minutes. Preheat the oven to 375 degrees. Bake the bread 25 minutes or until golden, and cut into wedges. Serves 12 to 16.

Skillet Corn Bread

This spicy skillet bread, sparked with both green and red chiles, is best served hot from the oven.

1 cup yellow cornmeal
1/2 cup all-purpose flour
2 Tbs. sugar
1/2 tsp. salt
1/2 tsp. baking soda
1/2 tsp. baking powder
1 Tbs. Chimayó chile powder
1 cup buttermilk
2 large eggs, beaten
2 fresh green New Mexico or other
   green chiles, roasted, peeled,
   seeded, and diced

1 fresh red jalapeño chile, seeded,
   and minced
1 red bell pepper, roasted, peeled,
   seeded, and diced
1 cup mild cheddar cheese, shredded
1/2 lb. cooked ham, finely diced
4 Tbs. unsalted butter

Preheat the oven to 400 degrees. In a large mixing bowl, whisk together the cornmeal, flour, sugar, salt, baking soda, baking powder, and chile powder. Pour the buttermilk and eggs into the dry mixture and stir to combine. Add the chiles, red pepper, and cheese to the batter and mix thoroughly. In a medium cast iron skillet, cook the ham in butter until it is nicely browned. Pour the ham and butter from the skillet into the batter and stir, then pour the batter back into the hot skillet and set on the center rack of the preheated oven. Bake the corn bread until it is firm and crusty, 30 to 40 minutes. Remove from the oven and turn out on a rack to cool, or cut into wedges straight from the skillet. Serves 8 to 12.

Desserts

Audrey's Ancho Apricot Cheesecake

Audrey's cheesecake can be made days or weeks in advance. Well-wrapped in plastic, it keeps in the refrigerator for up to 2 weeks, or in the freezer for up to 6 months.

$^1/_4$ cup butter, melted
2 cups crushed vanilla wafers
1$^1/_2$ lbs. fresh cream cheese
2 cups sugar
1 tsp. pure vanilla extract
1 Tbs. freshly squeezed lemon juice
4 large eggs

2 cups sour cream
7 Tbs. pure apricot preserves
2 tsp. Chimayó chile powder
   (see page 16)
5 Tbs. ancho chile puree
3 Tbs. dried apricots, finely diced

Preheat the oven to 350 degrees. Combine the butter and vanilla wafers and press the mixture into the bottom and halfway up the sides of a 10-inch springform pan. Wrap the bottom and sides of the pan tightly in heavy duty aluminum foil, and bake the crust at 350 degrees for 10 minutes. Remove the pan to cool on a rack, and reduce oven heat to 300 degrees.

In a large mixing bowl, cream the cheese with the sugar until thoroughly combined, then add the vanilla and lemon juice and mix well. Add the eggs one at a time, combining thoroughly after each addition. Mix in the sour cream, and pour the cheese batter into the cooled crust. In a small bowl, thoroughly combine 4 tablespoons apricot preserves, Chimayó chile powder, and 3 tablespoons ancho chile puree. Gently pour a pool of the apricot-chile puree into the center of the cheese batter. Using a long, narrow knife or a cake spatula, carefully swirl the apricot-chile mixture evenly through the cheese batter, taking care not to disturb the crust!

Bake the cheesecake at 300 degrees for 1 hour. Turn the oven off and leave the cheesecake in the closed oven for 1 hour. Remove the cheesecake from the oven and cool on a rack at room temperature for 1 hour or until thoroughly cool. Combine the remaining apricot preserves and ancho puree in a small bowl and drizzle the glaze over the cheesecake; sprinkle with finely diced dried apricots. Refrigerate the cheesecake to chill thoroughly before slicing. Serves 12 to 16.

Spicy Red Chile Gingerbread

Santa Fe artist Irene McAndrews came up with this dense, fragrant gingerbread. It's wonderful as is, or can be cut into layers and filled with pastry cream or sweetened cream cheese and nuts.

$1^1/4$ cups rye or rice flour
$1^1/4$ cups cornstarch
2 tsp. baking soda
1 tsp. cinnamon
$1/4$ tsp. ground cloves
$1/2$ tsp. ground ginger
$1^1/2$ tsp. Chimayó chile powder

$1/2$ cup granulated sugar
1 cup molasses
$1/2$ cup butter, softened
1 cup boiling water
2 eggs, beaten well
Powdered sugar

Preheat the oven to 325 degrees. Butter a 9-inch round cake pan. In a large bowl, sift the flour, cornstarch, baking soda, ground spices, and chile powder together several times; then stir in the sugar. Add the molasses and softened butter to the dry ingredients and mix thoroughly with an electric mixer. Add the boiling water in a stream, beating to incorporate; then add the eggs and mix until the batter is smooth. Pour the batter into the prepared pan, and bake at 325 degrees about 30 to 40 minutes. Set the pan on a rack for 10 minutes. Remove the cake from the pan to cool on the rack. Dust the top of the cake with powdered sugar before cutting. Serve warm or at room temperature with flavored whipped cream, or a fresh fruit sauce. Serves 8.

Brown Sugar Cookies with Chile Pecans

These crisp cookies are also good made with chile-spiced almonds or macadamia nuts. For extra richness, substitute chopped bittersweet chocolate for half the nuts called for in the recipe.

1/2 cup unsalted butter, softened
1 cup dark brown sugar
1 large egg
1 tsp. Mexican vanilla
1 1/4 cups all-purpose flour

1/2 tsp. baking soda
1/2 tsp. salt
1 cup Chile-Spiced Nuts (pecans),
   chopped (page 33)

Preheat the oven to 350 degrees, and butter a heavy baking sheet. Cream the butter and sugar together thoroughly in a large bowl. Add the egg and vanilla and mix on low speed until thoroughly combined. Sift the flour, baking soda, and salt together, and add to the butter mixture, mixing well. Stir in the chopped Chile-Spiced Pecans. Drop the batter by teaspoons onto the prepared baking sheet, about 2 inches apart. Bake the cookies for 12 to 15 minutes until nicely browned. Leave them on the baking sheet for about 2 minutes; then remove to a rack to cool. Makes about 30 cookies.

Pasilla-Poached Pears
with Orange Custard Sauce

The touch of mild red chile in this recipe complements the pears and sweet orange custard sauce.

1 cup dry red wine
1 cup sugar
Zest of half an orange,
   cut in julienne strips
1 stick cinnamon
2 whole cloves
1/2 pasilla chile, stemmed, seeded,
   and soaked
2 large, ripe Bartlett pears, peeled,
   halved, and cored

4 egg yolks
1/2 cup superfine sugar
1 3/4 cups boiling milk
1 tsp. Mexican vanilla
1 Tbs. Grand Marnier
   or other orange liqueur
4 large fresh mint leaves,
   for garnish

Put the red wine and sugar in a large, heavy saucepan and bring to a simmer, stirring until the sugar is dissolved. Add the orange zest, cinnamon stick, cloves, chile, and pears to the saucepan, adding water if necessary so that the pears are just covered by the liquid. Bring to a simmer, turn the heat low, and simmer the pears gently until they are tender, about 15 to 20 minutes. Remove the saucepan from the heat and let the pears cool in the syrup, then cover and chill.

In a large bowl, beat the egg yolks and add the superfine sugar gradually, beating 3 or 4 minutes until all the sugar is incorporated and the mixture is pale yellow and thickened. Continue beating while *slowly* dribbling the boiling milk into the yolks. Pour the mixture into a heavy, enameled saucepan and cook over medium-low heat, stirring slowly but constantly, until the sauce thickens to a light custard, about 8 minutes. *Do not let the sauce get near the simmer, or the yolks will separate.* Take the saucepan off the heat, set it in a sink or pan of cold water, and whisk until cool. Beat in the vanilla and Grand Marnier, cover and chill. Before serving, bring the pears to room temperature, then remove them from their syrup with a slotted spoon and drain on paper towels. Spoon 1/4 of the chilled orange custard into each of 4 deep dessert plates. Carefully place a pear half on top of the sauce in each plate, cut side down, and tuck a mint leaf under the pear at the stem end. Serves 4.

Mexican Chocolate Espresso Cake with Chile Mocha Sauce

This spicy, rich cake should be made at least 1 day ahead of serving. If you are unable to buy Mexican sweet chocolate tablets, substitute 6 ounces of sweetened or semi-sweet chocolate and add 1/8 teaspoon of ground cinnamon to the sugar in this recipe. Both Mexican chocolate and piloncillo (cones of Mexican raw sugar) can be obtained from the Santa Fe School of Cooking. The cake can be chilled, removed from the pan, wrapped tightly in plastic and foil, and frozen for up to 2 months.

2 tablets (6 oz.) Mexican sweet chocolate, chopped
10 oz. bittersweet chocolate, chopped
1 lb. unsalted butter, softened
3/4 cup piloncillo, chopped (or dark brown sugar)
1 1/4 cups espresso, freshly brewed
8 large eggs, beaten

1 cup heavy cream
1/2 Tbs. ancho or pasilla chile puree, or to taste (see page 16)
2 oz. Mexican sweet chocolate, grated
2 oz. bittersweet chocolate, grated
1 Tbs. powdered sugar
1/4 tsp. Chimayó chile powder

Preheat the oven to 350 degrees. Line a 9-inch-diameter cake pan (with high sides) with parchment paper. In a large glass or ceramic bowl set over a saucepan of gently boiling water, melt the chopped chocolates together, stirring occasionally until smooth. Remove the bowl of chocolate from the saucepan and set aside. In a heavy saucepan, bring the butter, piloncillo, and 1 cup espresso to a boil and gently simmer, stirring to dissolve sugar, for about 2 minutes. Pour the sugar mixture into the melted chocolate and whisk until smooth and cooled slightly. Whisk the eggs into the chocolate mixture to combine thoroughly, and pour the batter into the prepared pan. Place the cake pan in a deep-sided roasting pan, pour boiling water into the roasting pan to reach half way up the sides of the cake pan, and bake until the center of the cake is set, about 1 hour. Remove the pan from the water bath, cool on a rack, and refrigerate the cake at least 24 hours in the pan.

To make the Chile Mocha Sauce, pour the cream into a heavy saucepan and set over a medium-low flame. In a small bowl, stir the 1/4 cup espresso into the chile puree, then whisk the mixture into the chile-cream. Slowly bring the chile-cream mixture to a simmer and remove from heat. Immediately whisk in the grated chocolates and stir until the chocolate is melted. Taste for seasoning, and whisk in more chile puree if desired. Cover the saucepan and set aside (or chill up to 3 days, then bring to room temperature and warm over a very low flame, whisking until smooth).

To serve, remove the cake from the refrigerator and let sit at room temperature 15 minutes. With a sharp knife, cut around the sides of the pan to loosen the cake. Reverse a serving platter over the pan and invert the cake onto the platter, tapping the bottom of the pan gently until the cake is released. Lift off the pan, and peel the parchment paper from the cake. Let the cake stand 20 to 30 minutes to bring to room temperature. Mix the powdered sugar with the chile powder, then dust the cake with the mixture before slicing. Serve with warmed Chile Mocha Sauce on the side. Serves 16.

Orange Red Chile Flan

This version of the Mexican and southwestern favorite is mildly spiced with sweet red chile honey and flavored with orange.

1 cup sugar	7 egg whites
1 Tbs. Grand Marnier or other orange liqueur	4 egg yolks
1 tsp. Mexican vanilla	1 tsp. Mexican vanilla
3 cups milk	1/2 tsp. orange extract
1/2 cup red chile honey	1/2 tsp. ground cinnamon
1/4 tsp. salt	1 tsp. orange zest

Preheat the oven to 350 degrees. In a small, heavy saucepan combine the sugar, Grand Marnier, and vanilla and cook over low heat, stirring constantly, until the sugar is melted and the syrup is golden brown, about 10 minutes. Pour the hot syrup into a ring mold or 8-inch flan mold, and tilt the mold to coat the bottom and sides. Set the mold aside to cool. Stir together the milk, red chile honey, and salt. Beat in the egg whites and yolks and remaining ingredients until well blended. Pour the mixture through a sieve into the mold, set the mold in a deep roasting pan and pour boiling water into the pan to reach half way up the sides of the mold. Put the custard in the oven and bake about 50 minutes—when done, the center should still be a little soft. Remove the flan from the water bath and cool on a rack, then chill.

To unmold, loosen the edges of the flan carefully with a knife. Dip the mold into hot water for about 10 seconds to loosen the caramel, reverse a serving platter (with a rim) over the mold, and flip it over in one smooth, quick motion. Carefully remove the mold from the flan. Surround the flan with flavored whipped cream or fresh berries. Serves 8 to 10.

Chocolate Chile Lace Cookies

The lace cookies (which can be frozen for weeks, and recrisped in the oven before filling) may also be filled with jams, butter cremes, or ganache.

$1^1/2$ cups brown sugar
$1^1/2$ cups quick-cooking rolled oats
1 Tbs. flour
1 pinch salt
1 egg, lightly beaten

$2/3$ cup unsalted butter, melted
  and cooled slightly
8 oz. bittersweet chocolate
1 Tbs. ancho or pasilla chile puree,
  or to taste (see page 16)

Preheat the oven to 350 degrees. In a medium bowl, mix together the brown sugar, oats, flour, and salt. Stir in the egg and melted butter. Spoon the batter onto nonstick baking sheets (or cover sheets with baker's paper) by teaspoons, about 3 to 4 inches apart (they will spread). Bake until flat and golden brown, about 8 minutes. Cool the cookies on the baking sheets until crisp; they should pop off easily. In a glass bowl set over simmering water, melt the chocolate until smooth, and whip in chile puree to taste. When the cookies are thoroughly cooled, turn half of them over and drizzle the flat sides with warm chile-chocolate, then cover with the flat sides of the remaining cookies and press together. Makes about 20 filled cookies.

Creamy Pound Cake
with Red Chile Strawberry Sauce

Audrey's rich pound cake can be served alone or with this sweet-hot strawberry sauce. Wrapped tightly, the cake freezes beautifully.

3 cups fine cake flour
  (not self-rising)
2 sticks (1 cup) unsalted butter,
  softened
3 cups superfine sugar
7 large eggs, at room temperature
1 cup heavy cream

2 tsp. vanilla
1 pint fresh strawberries
2 tsp. dark rum
2 Tbs. powdered sugar
1 tsp. Chimayó chile powder,
  or to taste

Preheat the oven to 350 degrees. Butter and flour two loaf pans. Sift the flour twice and set aside. In a large mixing bowl, thoroughly cream the butter and sugar together until well combined. Add the eggs to the butter and sugar mixture one at a time, beating well after each addition. Beat half the flour into the batter; beat in the cream and vanilla; then beat in the remaining flour. Divide the batter between the two loaf pans, set them on a rack in the middle of the preheated oven, and bake for 45 minutes to 1 hour until a knife inserted at the center comes out clean. Leave the cakes in their pans for about 5 minutes, then turn out onto a rack to cool.

Wash, hull, and quarter the strawberries, and reserve half in a small bowl. In another bowl, sprinkle the remaining strawberries with the rum, powdered sugar, and chile powder, and mash to a coarse puree or pulse in a food processor. Set the strawberry puree aside at room temperature, stirring occasionally, for 10 or 15 minutes until the sugar has dissolved. Serve slices of pound cake drizzled with red chile strawberry sauce and topped with sliced fresh berries. Serves 4 to 6 (with lots of cake left over!).

Raspberry-Red Jalapeño
Cheesecake with Chocolate Crust

This elegant cheesecake, swirled through with raspberry-chile, keeps in the freezer for up to six months.

1/4 cup butter, melted
2 cups chocolate wafers,
    finely crushed
2 cups sugar
1 1/2 lbs. cream cheese, softened
1 tsp. pure vanilla extract

1 Tbs. freshly squeezed lemon juice
4 large eggs
2 cups sour cream
6 Tbs. pure raspberry preserves
1 tsp. red jalapeño chile powder

Preheat the oven to 350 degrees. Thoroughly mix the melted butter into the crushed chocolate wafers and press the mixture onto the bottom and half-way up the sides of a 10-inch springform pan. Wrap the bottom and sides of the pan in heavy-duty foil (to keep butter from dripping onto the bottom of the oven), and bake the crust at 350 degrees for 10 minutes. Remove the pan from the oven and cool on a rack. Reduce the oven temperature to 300 degrees.

For the filling, cream the sugar with the softened cream cheese until the mixture is smooth and fluffy. Mix in the vanilla extract and lemon juice, then add the eggs one at a time and combine thoroughly. Finally, add the sour cream, mix well, and pour the batter into the cooled chocolate shell. In a small bowl combine the raspberry preserves and red jalapeño chile powder; pour the raspberry-chile puree onto the center of the cheesecake batter. Using a knife or cake spatula, carefully swirl the raspberry-chile puree evenly through the batter, taking care not to disturb the crust!

Bake the cheesecake at 300 degrees for 1 hour. Turn the oven off, and leave the cheesecake in the closed oven for 1 hour; then remove from the oven and cool the cheesecake on a rack at room temperature until thoroughly cool. Refrigerate the cheesecake in the pan until it is thoroughly chilled before slicing. Serves 12 to 16.

Red Chile Caramel Parfait

Try this easy dessert with butter pecan or chocolate ice cream, or a combination.

1¹/₄ cups brown sugar
¹/₈ tsp. salt
¹/₂ cup light corn syrup
1¹/₂ cups heavy cream
1 tsp. vanilla

¹/₂ tsp. Chimayó chile powder
¹/₂ gallon vanilla ice cream,
  slightly softened
¹/₂ cup Chile-Spiced Nuts
  (page 33), finely chopped

In a heavy saucepan, stir together the sugar, salt, corn syrup, and 1 cup of cream. Set the saucepan over medium heat, bring to a boil, and boil *without stirring* to 240 degrees on a candy thermometer. Remove the sauce from the heat and stir in the remaining cream, the vanilla, and chile powder. Cool the sauce completely, cover and chill until ready to use.

To assemble the parfaits, let the chile caramel sauce stand at room temperature about 30 minutes. Spoon some of the softened ice cream into 6 parfait glasses and put them in the freezer to firm up. Spoon caramel sauce over the ice cream layer, then add more ice cream. Continue layering until the parfait glasses are filled. Sprinkle the parfaits with chopped spiced nuts. Serves 6.

Where to Buy Chiles

The red chile products used in these recipes are widely available in supermarkets and specialty stores in major metropolitan areas around the country. If you have difficulty finding chiles in your locality, call one of these reliable sources. Many of them provide regular mail order services.

SOUTHWEST

Bueno Foods
2001 Fourth Street SW
Albuquerque, NM 87102
505-243-2722
www.buenofoods.com

Casados Farms
P.O. Box 1269
San Juan Pueblo, NM 87566
505-852-2433

Chile Addict
325 Eubank NE
Albuquerque, NM 87123
505-237-9070
www.chileaddictstore.com

Chile Hill Emporium
P.O. Box 685
Placitas, NM 87043
505-867-3294

The Chile Shop
109 East Water Street
Santa Fe, NM 87501
505-983-6080
www.thechileshop.com

Chile Traditions
8204 Montgomery Blvd. NE
Albuquerque, NM 87109
505-888-3166
www.chiletraditions.com

Los Chileros
P.O. Box 6215
Santa Fe, NM 87501
505-471-6967
www.888eatchile.com

Chili Pepper Emporium
#89 Winrock Center
Albuquerque, NM 87110
505-881-9225
www.chilipepperemporium.com

Coyote Cocina
1590 San Mateo Lane
Santa Fe, New Mexico 87505
800-866-HOWL

Jane Butel's Cooking School Pantry
125 Second Street NW
Albuquerque, NM 87102
1-800-472-8229
www.janebutel.com

Leona's Foods, Inc.
P.O. Box 640
Moriarty, NM 87035
1-800-4LEONAS

Pecos Valley Spice Co.
400 Gold SW, Suite 500
Albuquerque, NM 87102
1-800-473-TACO (8226)
www.pecosvalley.com

Pendery's
1221 Manufacturing Street
Dallas, Texas 75207
1-800-533-1870
www.penderys.com

Santa Fe School of Cooking
116 West San Francisco Street
Santa Fe, NM 87501
505-983-4511
www.santafeschoolofcooking.com

Velardi's Chile Products
Emily & Roman Velardi
612 East Camino del Pueblo
Bernalillo, NM 87004
505-867-3027

WEST & NORTHWEST

Casa Lucas Market
2934 Twenty-Fourth Street
San Francisco, CA 94110
415-826-4334

La Palma
2884 Twenty-Fourth Street
San Francisco, CA 94110
415-647-1500

EAST

Dean and Deluca
560 Broadway
New York, NY 10012
212-226-6800
www.deandeluca.com

The Hot Shoppe
311 S. Clinton St.
Syracuse NY 13202
1-888-468-3287 (HOTEATS)
www.hotshoppe.com

Mo Hotta—Mo Betta
P.O. Box 1026
Savannah, GA 31402
1-800-462-3220
www.mohotta.com

Recipe List

Appetizers

Broiled Oysters Pasilla, 32
Chile-Spiced Nuts, 33
Chipotle Chicken Empanaditas, 34
Chipotle Fried Onion Rings, 34
Chunky Fresh Guacamole, 35
Nachos Nuevo Mexico, 36
Red Chile Balsamic Onions, 38
Red Chile Honey Baked Brie in Filo Crust, 32
Red Chile Olive Quesadillas, 37
Red Jalapeños Rellenos, 39
Red Pork Picadillo, 40
Red-Hot Queso, 41
Shrimp Cakes, 42
Smoky Chipotle Trout Pâté, 43
Smoky Stewed Garlic, 44

Breads

Blue Corn Muffins with Chile-Spiced Pecans, 136
Chile Pita Crisps, 137
Chile-Spiced Pumpkin Bread, 137
Jalapeño Cheese Corn Biscuits, 138
Red Chile Blue Cheese Focaccia, 140
Red Chile Cumin Wafers, 139
Red Chile Potato Bread, 141
Red Chile Scallion Dropped Biscuits, 139
Skillet Corn Bread, 142

Desserts

Audrey's Ancho Apricot Cheesecake, 144
Brown Sugar Cookies with Chile Pecans, 146
Chocolate Chile Lace Cookies, 150
Creamy Pound Cake with Red Chile Strawberry Sauce, 151
Mexican Chocolate Espresso Cake with Chile Mocha Sauce, 148
Orange Red Chile Flan, 149
Pasilla-Poached Pears with Orange Custard Sauce, 147
Raspberry-Red Jalapeño Cheesecake with Chocolate Crust, 152
Red Chile Caramel Parfait, 153
Spicy Red Chile Gingerbread, 145

Eggs & Cheese

Chama Camp Soufflé with Chile-Cinnamon Honey Butter, 80
Chimayó Chile Cheese Casserole, 81
Chipotle Shirred Eggs and Artichokes, 85
Christmas Hash, 82
Hot Cheese and Portabello Sandwich with Chipotle Mayonnaise, 87
Huevos Rancheros San Miguel, 86
Red Chile Omelette, 88
Red Polenta with Chiles and Cheese, 84
Spicy Southwestern Quiche, 89
Spinach and Trout Enchiladas Benedict, 83

Fish & Shellfish

Ancho Chile Crab Cakes, 92
Chile-Buttered Shrimp, 94
Chile-Crusted Tuna Wasabi, 94
Chile-Rubbed Catfish with Southwest Remoulade, 93
Cold Poached Salmon with Orange Chipotle Cream, 99
Fiery Red Snapper with Fennel, 96
New Mexico Chile-Smoked Salmon, 97
Pan-Fried San Juan Trout, 98
Pasilla Striped Bass Baked with Spinach, 95
Savory Boiled Shrimp with Jalapeño Salsa, 101
Scallops with Chile Pistachio Pesto, 100
Three-Chile Roasted Grouper, 102

Meats

Ancho Apricot Glazed Pork Chops, 118
Ancho Chile Glazed Lamb Shanks, 122
Audrey's Chile Barbecue Brisket, 114
Chile Blue Cheese Crusted Steak, 114
Chipotle Flank Steak, 117
Christmas Ham, 121
Grilled Steak with Guajillo Chile Sauce, 116
High Plains Meatballs, 118
Pork with Chile Colorado, 119
Rib Eye Steak with Wild Mushrooms, 115
Whiskey-Glazed Chile Ribs, 120

Pasta, Beans, and Rice

Ancho Rice Pilaf, 134
Black Bean Cakes, 130
Black Bean Refritos, 128
Borracho Baked Beans, 128
Chimayó Chicken and Penne Casserole, 126
Linguine with Ancho Gorgonzola Sauce, 125
New Mexico Ranch Beans, 127
Red Macaroni and Cheese, 124
Southwest Red Beans and Rice, 131
Spicy Pasilla Risotto with Roasted Red Pepper, 133
Spicy Spanish Rice, 132

Poultry

Chicken Albondigas, 112
Chile-Glazed Roast Cornish Game Hens, 111
Clay-Baked Red Duck, 104
Curried Slippery Chicken with Red Chile Peanut Sauce, 108
Herbed Chimayó Smoked Chicken, 110
Poblanos Rellenos with Turkey Picadillo, 105
Quick Turkey Mole, 106
Red Chile Fried Chicken, 109
Savory Stuffed Chicken Breasts, 107

Salads

Chile Caribe Chicken Salad, 62
Citrus and Scallion Salad with Chile-Glazed Piñon Nuts, 58
Fresh Fruit Salad with Spicy Avocado Dressing, 65
Gingered Chile Slaw, 63
Jícama, Apple, and Asiago Slaw with Ancho Chile Mayonnaise, 58
Roasted Beef and Field Greens with Red Chile Vinaigrette, 64
Roasted Winter Vegetable Salad with Red Chile Vinaigrette, 60
Serious Southwestern Slaw, 62
Southwest Potato Salad, 61
Southwest Salad with Red Chile Blue Cheese Dressing, 66
Spinach Salad with Sautéed Feta, Wild Mushrooms,
    and Pasilla Chile Dressing, 59

Sauces, Salsas, and Relish

Chile Caribe Rub, 20
Chile-Cherry Glaze, 20
Chimayó Red Sauce, 27
Chipotle Hollandaise Sauce, 23
Cilantro Mint Salsa, 24
Dried Cherry Chipotle Relish, 24
Orange Sauce with Chiles and Ginger, 25
Pasilla Chile Sauce with Almonds, 26
Red Chile Barbecue Sauce, 30
Red Chile Ginger Gremolata, 22
Red Chile Pear Chutney, 22
Roasted Garlic Chile Mayonnaise, 23
Salsa Fresca, 25
San Miguel Red Sauce, 28
Santa Cruz Red Sauce, 29
Smoky Barbecue Sauce, 30
Sweet Chipotle Vegetable Relish, 21

Soups and Stews

Chile Corn Chowder with Shrimp, 46
J. W. Hansel's Chile Con Carne, 50
New Mexico Tortilla Soup, 51
Pumpkin Soup with Chipotle Chile, 47
Red Chile Beef Stew, 52
Red Chile Posole, 48
Roasted Pepper and Corn Soup, 53
Spicy Shrimp Broth, 49
Tomato Chile Soup, 54
Veracruz Chowder, 55

Vegetables

Baked Red Chile Sweet Yams, 69
Chile Corn Pudding, 78
Chile Scalloped Potatoes with Asiago and Sage, 71
Chile-Roasted Cauliflower, 73
Creamy Red Chile Posole, 72
Red Chile Carrots Cointreau, 73
Red Roasted Vegetable Skewers, 74
Roasted Scarlet Potatoes, 75
Sautéed Kale with Chile Balsamic Dressing, 75
Skillet Butternut Squash with Cilantro-Mint Salsa, 70
Sugar Peas with Orange Chile Butter, 76
Twice-Baked Red Jalapeño Potatoes, 68
Vegetable Chilaquilas, 77

About the Authors

Kathleen Hansel is a private caterer in Santa Fe. Hansel has lived and cooked in Mexico, Arizona, Texas and New Mexico for the last 16 years—collecting, adapting and creating red chile recipes along the way. She currently resides in Santa Fe.

Audrey Jenkins is a cook and specialty baker, and was owner and operator of "A Piece of Cake" New York Cheesecake Company in Santa Fe from 1987 to 1991. Jenkins has been dessert chef for Celebrations and other popular Santa Fe restaurants, and a private caterer in Santa Fe and New York.

Personal Recipes